THE BEST BIKE RIDES IN DELAWARE, MARYLAND, VIRGINIA, WASHINGTON, D.C., AND WEST VIRGINIA

Help Us Keep This Guide Up to Date

Every effort has been made by the author and editors to make this guide as accurate and useful as possible. However, many things can change after a guide is published—establishments close, phone numbers change, facilities come under new management, and so on.

We would love to hear from you concerning your experiences with this guide and how you feel it could be improved and be kept up to date. While we may not be able to respond to all comments and suggestions, we'll take them to heart and we'll also make certain to share them with the author. Please send your comments and suggestions to the following address:

The Globe Pequot Press
Reader Response/Editorial Department
P.O. Box 480
Guilford, CT 06437

Or you may e-mail us at:

editorial@globe-pequot.com

Thanks for your input, and happy travels!

THE BEST BIKE RIDES® IN DELAWARE, MARYLAND, VIRGINIA, WASHINGTON, D.C., AND WEST VIRGINIA

by

Trudy E. Bell
revised and updated by Patrick Gilsenan

The Globe Pequot Press

Guilford, Connecticut

Cover design: Saralyn D'Amato-Twomey
Cover photograph: © John Kelly/courtesy of Pearl Izumi
Map design: Erin E. Hernandez
Interior photos: p. 11 by Barbara Lloyd; p. 59 courtesty of Carroll
County Tourism Office; p. 133 courtesy of the Washington, D.C.,
Convention & Visitors Association; p.99 courtesy of Nancy Taylor;
p. 173 by Pamela "Sam" Withrow, Camera One.

Library of Congress Cataloging-in-Publication Data is
available.

ISBN: 0-7627-0485-3

Manufactured in the United States of America
First Edition/First Printing

About the Authors

Trudy E. Bell is an avid touring cyclist and a certified bicycle mechanic. She has taught an introductory course in bicycle touring at the South Orange–Maplewood Adult School in New Jersey and at the Learning Annex in New York City.

Either with groups or solo, she and her 1984 Univega Sport-Tour have cycled all over the Mid-Atlantic states and in Colorado, Utah, and California, including the length of Baja California. In addition, she commuted by bicycle on the streets of New York City for five years—about 6,000 miles.

A former editor of *Scientific American*, *Omni*, and *IEEE Spectrum* magazines in New York City, she is now a communications specialist for McKinsey & Co., Inc., in Cleveland, Ohio. She has a master's degree in the history of science (American astronomy) from New York University. Her articles on bicycling have been published in *Adventure Cyclist*, *Collier's Encyclopedia*, *The Encyclopedia of New York City*, *The New York Times*, *Bicycle USA*, *Essence*, *Science Probe*, and *The Bicyclist's Sourcebook* (edited by Michael Leccese and Arlene Plevin, Woodbine House, 1991). She is the author of *Bicycling around New York City: A Gentle Touring Guide* and *The Essential Bicycle Commuter*.

She lives with her husband, historian of science Dr. Craig B. Waff, and daughter Roxana.

Patrick Gilsenan is a cyclist and writer living, working, and riding in Washington, D.C. He is the Local Knowledge columnist for the Mid-Atlantic region for *Bike* Magazine.

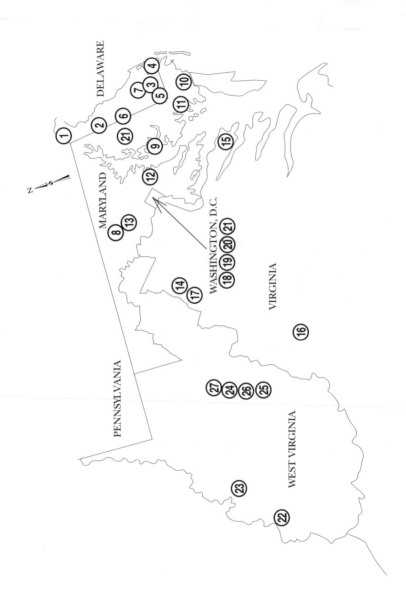

Contents

Introduction

Bike Rides

Appendix

Acknowledgments

This book and its previous editions would not be possible without the selfless dedication of scores of cyclists willing to work and share their knowledge.

But the greatest thanks go to the dozens of volunteers with whom I have worked closely over the months to find, verify, and fine-tune the rides presented here. Some volunteers spent time designing new rides while others devoted weekends to checking the accuracy of road signs, mileages, and businesses that may or may not have shut down since the last editions.

We want especially to thank those volunteers, including Bill Siwak of the Baltimore Bicycle Club, Karen and Tom Hartley of Delaware, Bill Davis of Delaware, Connie Garnett of West Virginia, and Gil Willis of the Elk River Touring Center in Slatyfork, West Virginia, who helped design new routes and who graciously fielded question after question to make sure the information was clear and accurate.

Our appreciation also goes to Mike Arnette of Old Dominion Bicycle Tours in Virginia, who took as much time and care verifying old rides as he did contributing new routes.

A special thanks also to Bruce and Alfreda Clinton of Delaware, Dennis Stawn of West Virginia, and Joseph Gilbert of Maryland, all of whom came through in the clutch on more than one ride.

We also want to thank John Fieseler, executive director of the Tourism Council of Frederick; Frank Pondolfina, David Shakelford, Nancy Estilow, and Gilbert Turner of Delaware; Nancy McComb of the Pocahontas County Tourism Office; Tony O'Leary and Betty Carver of the West Virginia Department of Tourism; and Jim Saulters of West Virginia.

Introduction

The green and rolling states of Delaware, Maryland, Virginia, Washington, D.C., and West Virginia make this part of the Mid-Atlantic one of America's prime cycling destinations. Whether you prefer the tough climbs of West Virginia, the easy rides of Delaware's seashore, or the rolling hills of Virginia's countryside, this area offers cycling opportunities for riders of all skill and fitness levels.

Despite rapid development of the nation's open spaces and its ever-growing network of highways, the Mid-Atlantic region—largely through the efforts of dedicated local clubs and regional cycling associations—has preserved many of the best cycling routes. Routes have been improved by wider shoulders along new roads and by the addition of signs guiding cyclists to the next turn. Many excellent secondary roads—once mere dirt tracks connecting farming communities—remain lightly traveled but well maintained.

The result of this preservation and advocacy are rides that will take you to the monuments of the nation's capital; through the historic port of Annapolis, Maryland; around the Amish communities of middle Delaware; and past the traditional sailing vessels of Maryland's Eastern Shore.

With this book, you'll be able to check out the cheetahs at the National Zoo, explore Civil War history, delve deep into the East Coast's largest underground caverns, ride through historic Delaware neighborhoods, and stand under one of the seven natural wonders of the world at Virginia's Natural Bridge. You'll have the opportunity to ride two of the nation's oldest ferries, stay in historic bed and breakfasts, or—if you prefer—camp out under the stars.

There are both urban rides and rural rides, so you can pick and choose the style you prefer. In and around Washington, D.C., for example, you'll be among hundreds of pedestrians, cars, and other cyclists, all sharing roughly the same space. But out in West Virginia, your only contact with humanity could be exchanging hellos with a farmer gathering mail from his roadside mailbox.

The routes in this book were contributed by local bicycle clubs, state tourism bureaus, bicycle touring companies, and individual cycling advocates. I hope you enjoy their work as much as I have.

Something for Everyone

To help you choose the most appropriate ride for your fitness level and experience, each ride in this book is categorized by its distance and difficulty. *Rambles* are the easiest and shortest rides, designed for almost all riders. They are under 35 miles long and are generally flat or slightly rolling. *Cruises* are intermediate in both difficulty and distance. They range from 25 to 50 miles and are rolling with some moderate climbs. Riders should be in fairly good physical shape to tackle these rides. *Challenges* are tougher, especially if they are attempted in a single day. Riders should be in good shape and should ride regularly before attempting one of these routes. *Classics* are the ultimate. They are long and hard, designed to please expert cyclists looking to push their limits. Classics are at least 60 miles long and include steep, mountainous climbs.

Though classics and challenges can be difficult, they don't necessarily exclude less conditioned and experienced riders. These rides are categorized by their *greatest* distance and difficulty. Many of these tougher rides include shorter versions that will lower their category rating, or can be completed in more than one day. A 50-mile challenge, for example, can be ridden as two 25-mile rambles. Many of the routes also include numerous resting points, such as parks and historic sites, which can help ease the rides' overall difficulty. You should also read the individual ride descriptions; some of the longer rides are very flat (such as the 115.8-mile Southern Delaware Challenge), and can be ridden over a couple of days by cyclists of only moderate fitness and experience. There's something for everyone.

How To Use this Book

Each ride begins with a short description to give you a sense of the tour's character and some of its main attractions. The description usually outlines the route, provides contact information, points out unique elements of the ride, and mentions inns, campgrounds, and other lodging when necessary.

If you think you might enjoy a ride after reading the description, move to "The Basics" section. Here you will find more specific information about the ride's length, options for shortening the ride, and an assessment of the required skill level. Where possible, "The Basics" will also break down the miles between food, lodging, and rest rooms. Some isolated routes may provide facilities only once or require you to bring your own provisions.

Once you've decided on a ride, you should become familiar with the "Miles & Directions" section. This section—known to riders as a cue sheet—is the nuts and bolts of the ride. It will tell you where and when to turn, how far to travel on a particular road, and when you are passing points of interest. It's important to read the cue sheet and the map before beginning your ride because the mileage directions can be complex or come in rapid succession. It's good to know roughly where you are before you start.

Whenever possible, the cue sheets use universal language, such as "T intersection," in which the road you are on dead-ends into a perpendicular road, and "fork" or "Y in the road," in which the road you are on splits in two directions.

You don't need a bike computer, which keeps track of miles traveled, to use the cue sheets. The mileages are given simply to help you navigate the route. For instance, when the next turn should be a quarter-mile up the road, but you have been riding for twenty minutes, you know you've gone too far.

The maps provided in each chapter will help you stay on course, but it's also wise to bring a local map showing the side and secondary roads. Should you lose your way, you can use the local maps to find your way back to the main route. A local map is also recommended because new construction can alter original routes and you will need some local knowledge to navigate your way around the obstruction.

A Word about this New Edition

Over the last few years, American cycling has soared in popularity. The federal government has enacted two transportation bills devoting more money to cycling over the next six years than has been spent in the last century. The result is wider shoulders on many roads, the designation of state bicycle and pedestrian coordinators, and better maps and facilities for cyclists.

We have also seen, however, increased development and the encroachment of urban sprawl on once-quiet country roads. Many roads and their corresponding bicycle routes have been closed, rerouted, or fundamentally changed in their character. The West Virginia Williams River Trail Cruise, for instance, which was included in the second edition, is no longer rideable and has been removed from this new edition. Traffic has increased to such a dangerous degree along Virginia's Stanley to New Market ride that the route needed to be radically altered for this edition.

The most important change for this edition, however, is that the old second edition *Best Bike Rides: Mid-Atlantic States*, has been split into two volumes in order to accommodate new rides and more detailed information. One volume covers the best rides in New York, Pennsylvania, and New Jersey. This volume encompasses the southern tier of the Middle Atlantic region, including Delaware, Maryland, northern Virginia, West Virginia, and the District of Columbia.

Among this edition's new rides are the Amish Country Challenge, which showcases central Delaware, and the Washington, D.C., Neighborhoods Ramble, which offers a side of the city not included in most tour guides. We have also upped the ante for the experienced, conditioned cyclist with the West Virginia Mountain Classic, which features some of the state's toughest climbs and most majestic views. Every ride included from the second edition has been updated and verified with the latest contact information and news of new attractions and accommodations. These updates are the result of the hard work of dozens of cycling advocates who shared their local knowledge to provide a more pleasant riding experience for others who know the joy of the road. To these stalwart volunteers I give my heartfelt thanks. Keep riding!

A Special Word about West Virginia

West Virginia provides some of the most breathtaking scenery in the Mid-Atlantic region. Its soaring mountains, hidden valleys, and untouched villages make the state a true cycling adventure. It is, however, as difficult to ride as it is beautiful.

In addition to its tough climbs, the state is sparsely populated and there are long, lonely stretches without food, water, or rest rooms. Many of the main and secondary roads include miles-long climbs at eight- or nine-percent grades—very steep. And the flip side of those climbs are long and extremely fast downhill sections that can be dangerous for inexperienced cyclists. While other rides in the region, such as Virginia's New Market to Luray tour, feature nine-percent grades, West Virginia's combination of distance and grades makes this state's routes especially difficult.

Although many of West Virginia's back roads are lightly traveled and well maintained, the main roads are often narrow and without shoulders. Cars and big trucks zip by at 55 miles per hour or more. Also, many roadsides are covered with gravel, which can be dangerous stuff when it spills into the roadway. The secondary roads, however, often have so little motorized traffic that you should have plenty of time to react to gravel, downhill turns, and other obstacles.

The most demanding West Virginia ride in this book is the West Virginia Mountain Classic, which includes a trip along scenic Highway 150. The 23-mile section through the Monongahela National Forest has few services other than primitive campgrounds— and there are severe variations in elevation. The payoff is a beautiful ride framed by the state's characteristic sharp mountain ridges, reminiscent of Virginia's Blue Ridge Parkway. This ride, however, is one of the few that we recommend only for experienced and conditioned cyclists.

The West Virginia Inn to Inn Cruise is a mountainous ride that can be completed by the casual cyclist. This route offers pleasant mountain views but is short, lightly traveled, and is more rolling than steep. The rural atmosphere also allows riders to rest almost anywhere along the route.

West Virginia's mountains have made the state a mecca for mountain bikers, with plenty of touring companies that provide services for a safe and enjoyable trip. But when riding alone or with friends, be prepared to rough it. Bring the riding skills necessary for the route, the tools needed for basic repairs, and enough food and water to get you from one mountain town to the next. If you follow these simple suggestions, West Virginia cycling can be some of the most rewarding in the region.

For more information about the state's road and mountain biking opportunities call the West Virginia Division of Tourism, 800–225–5982.

A Word about Riding in Washington, D.C.

The nation's capital is a great place for bicycle touring. Great views and historic buildings are clustered within just a few square miles. The Washington rides in this book suit the city's compact geography, offering four quick and easy rides offering different views of the city.

The Washington Memorial Ramble is the most "official" of the D.C. rides, taking cyclists to the steps of the city's most famous structures. Riders will coast past the White House, the Jefferson and Lincoln Memorials, the White House, the Washington Monument, and the Supreme Court, to name just a few. It's a ride that can be completed in just a few hours or over the course of days as you explore different places along the route.

The Washington Bridges Ramble also features much of official Washington, but is a quicker and less complex ride. It showcases the city's waterfront, bridges, and Tidal Basin while offering more long-range views of the Mall's great buildings and monuments. This is the route for those seeking a pleasant bike ride rather than a history lesson.

The other two rides, the Washington Neighborhoods Ramble and the Rock Creek Park Cruise, take participants away from the city's most famous district. The Rock Creek Park Cruise features Washington's version of Central Park and showcases the wildlife and small waterway in the heart of this urban center. The Washington Neighborhoods Ramble is the least "monumental" of the D.C. rides, taking you into the neighborhoods where Washingtonians live and past the parks where they play. In a way it provides the most accurate portrayal of the nation's capital—a place where real people live, shop for groceries, and hunt for parking spaces.

The Neighborhood and Monument routes put riders in contact with some heavy traffic on congested urban streets, so be sure to review the descriptions before starting out. It's a good idea to check out the whole section on Washington before choosing your route; the four rides intersect at different points, allowing you to create your own capital tour.

Enjoy the city.

Safety and Comfort on the Road

Like any outdoor activity, cycling carries a certain amount of risk. Cycling includes speed, mingling with traffic, and the harsh reality of unforgiving blacktop.

Bicycle riding is, however, a safe, relatively low-injury sport that can be made even safer with the right technique and equipment.

Your most important piece of safety equipment is a helmet. Always wear a helmet, whether you are riding a century or just around the block. No matter how cautious you are, you will eventually fall off your bicycle. A good helmet may well be the difference between a scraped elbow and a trip to the emergency room. Helmets vary greatly in style and price, but a good helmet is one that fits comfortably, provides sufficient—and often adjustable—padding, and has openings for ventilation. Lighter-colored helmets reflect the sun's rays more effectively and are most visible at night. A well-fitting helmet will remain stationary on your head while you are riding; your chin strap should be firmly in place but not so tight that it restricts the movement of your head.

Cycling gloves aren't just for looks. Fingerless, padded gloves are extremely important on longer rides because they absorb the shock of the road and prevent the formation of blisters. Cycling is a gear-oriented sport and this is one item you could—but probably shouldn't—be without.

Other, optional gear includes padded shorts, cycling jerseys, and sunglasses. On longer rides padded shorts are almost essential. They reduce "saddle soreness," which is pain resulting from the soft tissue and bones of your sitting area absorbing the shock of the road. Equally important, however, is the ability of good padded shorts to prevent chafing—that painful rash that results when your thighs and backside rub against loose clothing or the bicycle seat. Chafing can turn an enjoyable ride into a painful endurance test. If chafing does occur, the cause and symptoms can sometimes be relieved by an application of Vaseline to the affected area. Gel seats, sheepskin seat covers, and sometimes just a change in the shape of the seat can also reduce chafing, depending on the size and shape of the rider.

Cycling jerseys, available at most bike shops, are a good idea because their bright colors increase visibility and their moisture-wicking properties help keep you cool and dry. Many jerseys are also equipped with back pockets, which are sometimes the best way to carry wallets, keys—or this book.

Like gloves, sunglasses are not just part of cycling fashion. Safe cycling depends on your ability to see ahead and react quickly. Even a moment of blindness at 20 miles per hour can be dangerous. So anything that increases your ability to see and makes you look cool in the process is probably a good idea.

Many touring cyclists also mount rearview mirrors on their helmets or sunglasses to allow them to see what is approaching from behind. This can be especially useful on busy urban streets.

A basic tool kit on a long ride is as essential as any piece of clothing. Few things can ruin a day as quickly, or be as dangerous, as being faced with a flat tire you can't repair 25 miles from the nearest phone. You don't have to be a certified bicycle mechanic or lug your entire workshop with you on the road. An air pump, patches or extra tube, tire levers, a chain rivet tool, and a few Allen wrenches are all you need for most roadside repairs. The tools can be mounted on your bike or carried in your pockets, or they will fit nicely into one of the latest cycling bags. There are now multipurpose tools that have virtually all of the essentials in one conveniently small package. Ask your bike-shop mechanic to recommend the tools that best fit your needs and components.

The final defense against injury and breakdown is just that: *defense*. Riding defensively is probably the best way to take control of your own experience. Defensive cycling is, first and foremost, being aware of your surroundings at all times and reacting appropriately. It's fun to look at the scenery, but not when your are pedaling just a couple of feet from 65-miles-per-hour traffic.

Always remember that bicycles are considered vehicles and must follow all federal and state laws applied to automobiles. That means stopping at stop signs and red lights, yielding right of way, using arm signals to indicate your movements, and using the left turn lane where appropriate. As a vehicle, however, you are entitled to your share of the road. If you do not feel safe riding near the edge of a roadway—which is where you should be whenever possible—you have a right to use as much of the road as necessary to insure your safety.

Other tips include keeping an eye out for hidden driveways, parked cars pulling into the street, or drivers about to open their car doors. A bell, which is required in many states, is a good way to warn others of your approach.

With these simple tools and techniques the routes in this book and the ones you find as you explore your own neighborhoods should prove to be safe and fun.

A Modest Request

Cycling, as is evident from the many clubs and advocacy organizations around the country, is a social sport. Because this book is an extension of that cycling community, I will be grateful to receive any suggestions, corrections, or additions other riders might have concerning the rides presented here. New rides or variations on the rides in this book are equally welcome. Please send changes or additions to The Globe Pequot Press, 246 Goose Lane, Suite 200, Guilford, Connecticut, 06437.

Delaware

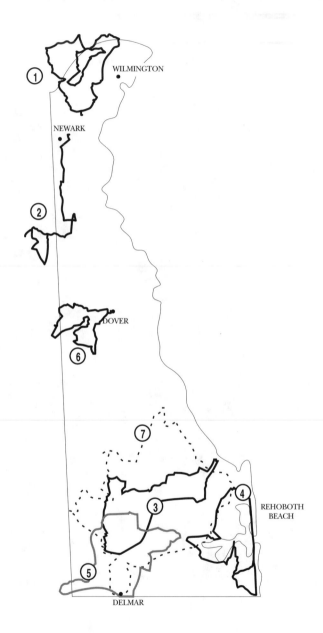

WILMINGTON

①

NEWARK

②

DOVER

⑥

⑦

③

④

REHOBOTH
BEACH

⑤

DELMAR

Delaware

1

Delaware—Pennsylvania Hill-Climbing Cruise

Delcastle Recreation Area—Kennett Square—
Cossart—Delcastle Recreation Area

This hilly, challenging ride along less traveled roads offers lovely forest and wooded area scenery, with many old homes of lots of historical character. You'll wander on backroads that the developers have not yet discovered, as you ride from the outskirts of Wilmington, Delaware (New Castle County), into Pennsylvania toward Philadelphia (Chester County). For the least traffic pedal early on a Saturday or Sunday morning, as some of the main two-lane roads do see heavier automobile traffic during the week, suggests David Shackleford, bicycle-commuter expert of Wilmington's White Clay Bicycle Club, who contributed the ride.

The route is shaped as if you were tracing the outline of the letter *V*. The longer 37-mile version dips down into the center of the *V* to include a stop at the Ashland Nature Center (302–239–2334), where you can stretch your legs on some nature trails. Then the ride continues by taking you through one of Delaware's few remaining covered bridges. The shorter 26.7-mile version eliminates the 10-mile dip down the center of the V-shaped route, turning the route into a simple triangle. Both rides take you near a second covered bridge.

About 9 miles into both the longer and the shorter versions of the ride, you'll pedal along the southern edge of Kennett Square, a small town whose downtown shopping district is quaint but whose outskirts have the typical convenience stores.

Because the ride takes less traveled roads, there are no services on the route itself; neither does the route pass any bike shops or bed-and-breakfast inns, although there are a number in the general area, Shackelford notes. The two covered bridges and the Ashland Nature Center offer scenic places to stop for a packed snack or lunch. Another good lunch stop is a rustic restaurant and bar called Buckley's Tavern in Centerville (5812 Kennett Pike, 302–656–9776), about 30 miles into the longer ride (about 20 miles into the shorter ride); if you plan to stop there, call ahead for the tavern's hours, which are somewhat limited. Another nice lunch stop is the Hoopes Reservoir, where you can sit and enjoy the view of the lake. Near the end of the route, you'll pedal by the Mount Cuba Astronomical Observatory (call 302–654–6407 for information on activities and public observing hours).

The Basics

Start: Millcreek, Delaware, at the public parking lot of the Delcastle Tennis Center at the north entrance to the Delcastle Recreation Area. During spring and summer, a portable toilet is located next to the parking lot near the tennis courts; water fountains are scattered throughout the recreation area. To get to the start, take Rte. 41 (Newport Gap Pike) to Millcreek Rd. Head west on Millcreek Rd. for 0.3 mile and turn left on McKennans Church Rd. into the Delcastle Recreation Area.

Length: 26.7 or 37 miles.

Terrain: Moderately hilly. Traffic is generally light on weekends, although during the week it can be moderate to moderately heavy on some main roads.

Food: Across from the Delcastle Tennis Center is the Delcastle Inn Restaurant, 801 McKennans Church Rd. (302–994–4600), at the Delcastle Golf Course. Open daily to the public for casual breakfast, lunch, and dinner from 7:00 A.M. to 9:30 P.M. Typical clientele are golfers so dress is casual. Other that that and Buckley's Tavern there are no convenience stores, restaurants, or water stops directly on the route, although detours of 1–2 miles will bring you plenty in Kennett Square and Chadds Ford. Pack your own snacks and water.

Miles & Directions

- 0.0   From the Delcastle Recreational Area/Tennis Center entrance, turn right onto McKennans Church Rd. (Rd. 276).
- 0.2   Turn left at the Red Clay Presbyterian Church onto unmarked Mill Creek Rd. (Rd. 282).
- 1.1   Bear right to continue on unmarked Mill Creek Rd. You are now on Delaware's Bicycle Route 1, a north-south bicycle route.
- 2.2   Turn right at the stop sign to continue on Mill Creek Rd.
- 4.2   Turn left at the T intersection onto unmarked Old Lancaster Pike (Rd. 300), followed by an immediate right onto unmarked Yorklyn Rd. (Rd. 257). Follow the green Bicycle Route 1 arrows.
- 4.3   Cross Lancaster Pike to continue straight on Yorklyn Rd. *Note: Convenience stores and delis are located within a few blocks in either direction on Lancaster Pike. It's a good place to stop and pick up snacks or drinks for the ride.*
- 4.8   Turn left onto Old Wilmington Rd. (Rd. 275). You leave Delaware Bicycle Route 1, which continues straight. As you climb Old Wilmington Rd., the circa 1730 Hockessin Friends Meeting building will be on your right.
- 5.2   At the bottom of the hill, bear right to continue on Old Wilmington Rd.

CHADDS
FORD

COSSART

KENNETT
SQUARE

Rosedale Rd.

For the 26.7-mile
ride, turn left;
for the 37-mile
ride, turn right

Cossart Rd.

Fairville Rd.

52

Kennett Pike

Chadds Ford Rd.

100

Montchanin Rd.

Hillendale Rd.

Norway Rd.

Center Mill Rd.

Hillendale Rd.

Kaolin Rd.

Burnt Mill Rd.

Burnt Mill Rd.

Nine Gates Rd.

Old Kennett Pike

Snuff Mill Rd.

Twaddell Mill Rd.

PENNSYLVANIA
(Chester County)

Lower Snuff
Mill Row

Old Kennett Pike

Kennett Pike

Chandlers
Mill Rd.

(New Castle County)
DELAWARE

Snuff Mill Rd.

Ashland Clinton School Rd.

52

82

Rte. 41

Old Wilmington Rd.

Sharpless Rd.

Ashland Nature
Center

Covered Bridge

New
London Rd.

Owls Nest Rd.

Yorklyn Rd.

Brackenville Rd.

Barley Mill Rd.

Mount Cuba Rd.

Hillside Mill Rd.

Old Wilmington Rd.

Old Lancaster Pike

Rte. 41

Hoopes
Reservoir

Millcreek Rd.

Deer Valley Ln.

Covered Bridge

Foxhill Ln.

Barley Mill Rd.

Rolling Mill Rd.

48

Lancaster Pike

N

Limestone
Hills Park

Millcreek Rd.

Hercules Rd.

START

Delcastle
Recreation Area

McKennans Church Rd.

- 6.2 Turn right onto Chandler Mill Rd. You have now entered Pennsylvania. Road names will be posted vertically on brown wooden posts.
- 6.7 At the bottom of the hill, bear right as Chandler Mill Rd. merges with Kaolin Rd. Then turn immediately left to stay on Chandler Mill Rd.
- 7.1 Turn right to stay on Chandler Mill Rd. and immediately cross a one-lane stone and metal bridge built in 1910. Read the marble marker on your left as you cross the bridge.
- 8.6 Turn right onto Hillendale Rd., which truly takes you over hill and dale and past a few of the many mushroom farms in the area.
- 9.4 At the five-corner intersection with the stop sign and flashing red light, continue straight across Kaolin Rd. to continue on Hillendale Rd. To visit Kennett Square's restaurants and shops (the area is promoted as the Mushroom Capital of the World), turn left and ride for about 1 mile.
- 12.1 Turn right onto Rosedale Rd., followed by an immediate right onto Norway Rd. You'll now be headed back in roughly the same direction you came.
- 12.8 Bear right to continue on Norway Rd.
- 13.5 Turn right at the T intersection onto Burnt Mill Rd.
  Note: For the 26.7-mile ride, at this T intersection turn left onto Burnt Mill Rd. At mile 13.9, turn left onto Center Mill Rd. and then resume following the directions at mile 24.7 below.
- 14.2 Bear right at the T intersection onto Old Kennett Pike.
- 14.3 Make your first left turn onto Nine Gates Rd. You have now reentered Delaware.
- 15.4 As you reach the stop sign at Lower Snuff Mill Row, bear left to stay on Nine Gates Rd. (Note: Delaware maps say Upper Snuff Mill Row, but the street sign says Lower Snuff Mill Row.)
- 15.5 Turn right at the T intersection onto Snuff Mill Rd. (Rd. 247).

- 15.6 Turn left at the T intersection onto unmarked Route 82 (Creek Rd.). You are now riding along Red Clay Creek. Use caution when approaching railroad crossings.
- 16.1 Turn right onto Sharpless Rd. (Rd. 251) and immediately cross Red Clay Creek. A waterfall will be on your right as you begin a 1-mile climb. At the top of the hill on your left will be a quaint old house circa 1840 and farther down you'll find a circa 1730 rock farmhouse and barn named Snug Hill.
- 17.6 Turn left onto Old Wilmington Rd. (Rd. 275).
- 18.4 Turn left onto unmarked Brackenville Rd. (Rd. 274).
- 19.5 Turn left onto Barley Mill Rd. Ahead will be a single-lane covered bridge. Immediately before the bridge is the Ashland Nature Center (302) 239–2334 where you'll find rest rooms and water fountains. The rest rooms, along with a nature store and library, are located in the main building behind the nature center residence. Hours are Monday through Friday, 8 A.M. to 4:30 P.M., Saturday 9 A.M. to 3 P.M. and Sunday noon to 4 P.M.
- 19.8 Immediately after crossing the railroad tracks, turn left at the T intersection onto Rte. 82 (Creek Rd.).
- 19.9 Make your first right onto Ashland Clinton School Rd. (Rd. 287).
- 21.4 Turn left at the T intersection onto Old Kennett Pike (Rd. 243).
- 21.6 Make your first right onto unmarked Snuff Mill Rd. (Rd. 244).
- 23.1 Turn left at the T intersection onto unmarked Rte. 52 (Kennett Pike). To visit Buckley's Tavern and other shops in Greenville, turn right and proceed along Kennett Pike. Buckley's will be on your right within half a mile.
- 23.6 Turn left onto Burnt Mill Rd. You're again in Pennsylvania. Note the Oberod Estate on your left. The twenty-four-room French country-style mansion, built in 1937 on a

forty-acre estate for Mr. and Mrs. Harry W. Lunger was donated to the Episcopal Diocese of Delaware in 1979. It is now a conference center.

■ 24.7 Turn right onto Center Mill Rd.

Note: It is at this intersection that the 26.7-mile ride rejoins the longer route. Those doing the 26.7-mile ride should turn left onto Center Mill Rd.

■ 25.6 Turn right onto Fairville Rd. While riding on Fairville Rd., you will cross Rte. 52 (Kennett Pike). Several antiques stores (but no food or drink) are immediately to your left in the historic town of Centerville on Rte. 52 (Kennett Pike).

■ 26.3 Turn right onto unmarked Crossert Rd. Enjoy the long downhills here; you'll pay for them later.

■ 26.4 At the intersection of Stockford Rd., continue straight on unmarked Crossert Rd. as the pavement narrows to one lane.

■ 28.0 Turn right at the T intersection onto unmarked Rte. 100 (Chadds Ford Rd.). Chadds Ford Rd. becomes Montchanin Rd. as you cross back into Delaware.

■ 28.7 Turn right onto unmarked Twaddell Mill Rd. (Rd. 234), where you'll begin the ride's most challenging climbs.

■ 30.0 A small park with picnic tables will be on your left before Rte. 52 (Kennett Pike). It's a good spot to take a breather, after those climbs.

■ 30.0 Continue straight on Owl's Nest Rd. (Rd. 240). The Owl's Nest Rd./Rte. 52 (Kennett Pike) is the center of the historic town of Centerville, containing several offices, boutique and antiques shops, and Buckley's Tavern (302–565–9776). The tavern welcomes cyclists and opens 11:30 A.M. Monday through Friday and 11:00 A.M. Sunday.

■ 32.1 Continue straight where Owl's Nest Rd. (Rd. 240) becomes New London Rd. and joins Rte. 82 North.

■ 32.4 make your first left onto Hillside Mill Rd. (Rd. 269). On this road you'll pass Hoopes Reservoir and the Mount Cuba Astronomical Observatory (302–654–6407).

- 33.2 Immediately after the railroad tracks, turn left onto un-marked Mt. Cuba Rd. (Rd. 261).
- 33.6 Turn left at the T intersection onto unmarked Barley Mill Rd. (Rd. 258). Watch for diagonal railroad crossings.
- 34.6 Turn right onto unmarked Rolling Mill Rd. (Rd. 263) and immediately cross Red Clay Creek with a small waterfall on your right. While on Rolling Mill Rd., as you pass Foxhill Ln., you'll see another covered bridge to your right.
- 35.2 Turn right at the T intersection onto Rte. 48 (Lancaster Pike).
- 35.4 Make your first left onto Hercules Rd. (Rd. 282), past Hercules Country Club and golf courses. The road becomes Mill Creek Rd. after crossing Rte. 41.
- 36.7 Turn left onto McKennans Church Rd. (Rd. 276).
- 37.0 Turn left back into the Delcastle Recreational Area/Ten-nis Center parking lot.

2

Two-State Breakfast Cruise

Newark—Chesapeake City—Newark

This 48-mile route from Newark, Delaware, to Chesapeake City, Maryland, has long been a popular "breakfast" ride with the White Clay Bicycle Club (WCBC), headquartered in Wilmington, Delaware. The destination: Jack and Helen's Restaurant (410–885–5477), a down-home diner that "serves really good, inexpensive breakfasts, sandwiches, and platters. Very "bicycle friendly," notes Nancy Waddell, former editor of WCBC's newsletter *Tailwind*, who contributed and updated the cue sheet on which this ride is based.

The ride starts at Casho Mill Barksdale Park near the Newark campus of the University of Delaware in New Castle County. At first you will pedal along some fairly busy roads, but they generally have wide shoulders. Soon you will cross Summit Bridge over the Chesapeake and Delaware Canal and pass through the Canal National Wildlife Area. The canal, which first opened to traffic in 1829, is now one of the busiest canals in the world, averaging more than 22,000 vessels a year; you may be lucky enough to see large, oceangoing freighters plying their way between Baltimore and Philadelphia.

Recent Delaware housing and commercial development has decreased the rural feel of this ride; however, the western Maryland section continues to provide a scenic loop through some of Cecil County's thoroughbred horse farms.

As you finish the outward leg, 27 miles into the ride, you'll undoubtedly have worked up quite an appetite. Chow down at Jack and Helen's, where the waitresses know everyone, as most of the patrons are locals. "Their pancakes are #1 on our list and are typically what we order," notes Waddell. Crowded on weekends, especially very early in the morning, Jack and Helen's is open before dawn seven days a week.

After remounting your bike, you can pause to let some of the feast digest by stopping less than a mile into the return to gaze at the exhibits in the Chesapeake & Delaware Canal Museum. The 21-mile return leads you back essentially along the outward route minus the scenic loop.

The Basics

Start: Newark, Delaware, at Casho Mill Barksdale Park, at the corner of Barksdale Rd. and Casho Mill Rd. Park cars in one of the three lots. In the summer there are portable toilets set up, but no water. From I-95 take Rte. 896 north along College Ave. South, Christina Pkwy., and Elkton Rd.; turn left onto Casho Mill Rd., right onto Barksdale Rd., and left into Casho Mill Barksdale Park.
Length: 48 miles.
Terrain: Flat to gently rolling. Recent housing and commercial development has created heavy traffic along portions of this ride; however, wide shoulders are provided on the main roads.
Food: Available near 1 mile and 6 miles into the ride and at Jack and Helen's at mile 27. But carry water and snacks, as there are some long stretches without services.

Miles & Directions

- 0.0   Turn right out of the parking lot of Barksdale Park.
- 0.2   Turn left at the traffic light onto Casho Mill Rd.

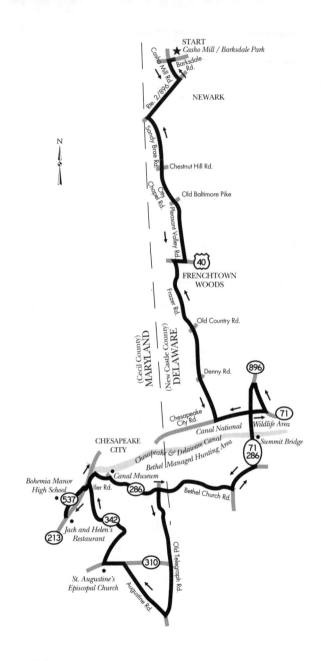

START
★ Casho Mill / Barksdale Park

Casho Mill Rd.

Barksdale Rd.

Rte. 2/896

NEWARK

Sandy Brae Rd.

Chestnut Hill Rd.

Otts Chapel Rd.

Old Baltimore Pike

Pleasant Valley Rd.

40

FRENCHTOWN WOODS

Frazer Rd.

Old Country Rd.

(Cecil County) MARYLAND

(New Castle County) DELAWARE

Denny Rd.

896

71

Wildlife Area

Chesapeake City Rd.

Canal National

71 286

Summit Bridge

CHESAPEAKE CITY

Chesapeake & Delaware Canal

Bethel Managed Hunting Area

Bohemia Manor High School

Canal Museum

537

Iler Rd.

286

Bethel Church Rd.

342

213

Jack and Helen's Restaurant

310

Old Telegraph Rd.

St. Augustine's Episcopal Church

Augustine Rd.

N

- 0.8   Turn right at the T intersection onto Rte. 2/896 (Elkton Rd.). Use caution; this road is busy but has wide paved shoulders. Be very careful in passing the shopping center on your right, watching for cars turning right. (This shopping center includes a grocery store and deli.)
- 2.0   Turn left at the traffic light onto Sandy Brae Rd. This road changes its name several times. After crossing Chestnut Hill Rd., it becomes Otts Chapel Rd. (Rd. 397). At mile 4.3, after crossing the Old Baltimore Pike, keep heading straight on Pleasant Valley Rd. (Rd. 8).
- 5.9   Turn right at the T intersection onto Rte. 40 (Pulaski Hwy.), watching carefully for cars. This road is busy but has a wide paved shoulder. (*Note:* If you were to turn left instead of right onto Rte. 40, you would reach a shopping center with a grocery store, deli, fast-food restaurants, and gas stations.
- 6.1   Take the first left onto Frazer Rd. (Rd. 391), a nice rural change of pace after busy Rte. 40. At mile 8.0, cross unmarked Old County Rd. At mile 9.4 cross Denny Rd. (Rd. 396).
- 10.5 Turn left at the T intersection onto Chesapeake City Rd.
- 11.8 Turn left at the T intersection onto Rte. 71 (Red Lion Rd.).
- 12.6 Turn left at the T intersection onto Rte. 71/896 (Summit Bridge Rd.), which is moderately busy but has wide paved shoulders that narrow when you reach Summit Bridge. Cross Summit Bridge over the Chesapeake and Delaware Canal.
- 14.7 Turn right onto Bethel Church Rd. (Rd. 433).
- 15.6 Turn right to stay on Bethel Church Rd. (Rd. 433) where Choptank Rd. continues straight. At the Maryland border Bethel Church Rd. changes its designation to Rte. 286.
- 17.6 Turn left onto Old Telegraph Rd. At mile 19.5 keep heading straight at the stop sign at the unmarked intersection with Rte. 310 (Cayots Corner Rd.).
- 20.8 Make a sharp right onto Augustine Rd. (the sign says St. Augustine, although the maps say Augustine).

- 22.5 Turn left at the T intersection onto Rte. 310 (Cayots Corner Rd.).
- 23.1 Turn right at St. Augustine's Episcopal Church onto Rte. 342 (St. Augustine Rd. N.).
- 25.9 Turn left onto unmarked Iler Rd.; watch carefully, for this turn is easy to miss. Immediately cross Rte. 286 and pass under the very high bridge of Rte. 213. At mile 26.7 head straight onto unmarked Rte. 537 (Basil Ave.).
- 27.0 Bear left at the Bohemia Manor High School to stay on Rte. 537 (Basil Ave.). Cross Rte. 213 to Jack and Helen's Restaurant for a well-deserved breakfast. Leave the restaurant parking lot by turning right to head north on Rte. 213.
- 27.9 Bear right onto Rte. 286.
- 28.4 Turn right at the deli to stay on Rte. 286 (here called 2nd St.) On parallel 1st Street, 1 block away, is the "main drag" of South Chesapeake City, with quaint shops, a bed-and-breakfast inn, a fancy restaurant on the water, and other amenities.
- 28.9 Turn right at the T intersection to stay on Rte. 286. The Chesapeake & Delaware Canal Museum is across the road to your left. At mile 30.3 you'll pass Old Telegraph Rd., and then you'll leave Maryland and reenter Delaware. At the border Rte. 286 becomes Bethel Church Rd. (Rd. 433).
- 32.3 Turn left at the stop sign to stay on Bethel Church Rd. (Rd. 433).
- 33.1 Turn left at the blinking light onto Rte. 71/896 (Summit Bridge Rd.), watching carefully for traffic.
- 35.2 Turn right onto Rte. 71 (Red Lion Rd.).
- 36.0 Bear right onto Chesapeake City Rd.
- 37.3 Make the first right onto unmarked Frazer Rd. (Rd. 391).
- 41.7 Turn right at the T intersection onto Rte. 40, watching carefully for traffic.
- 42.0 Take the first left at the traffic light onto Pleasant Valley Rd. (Rd. 8), which changes its name first to Otts Chapel Rd. (Rd. 387) and then to Sandy Brae Rd.

- 45.9 Turn right at the T intersection onto Rte. 2/896 (Elkton Rd.), watching carefully for traffic.
- 47.1 Turn left onto Casho Mill Rd. Caution! This intersection is busy. If you happen to miss the turn, you'll know it because the paved shoulder disappears.
- 47.7 Turn right at the traffic light onto Barksdale Rd.
- 47.9 Turn left into the parking lot of Casho Mill Barksdale Park.

3

Inn-to-Inn Triangle Three-Day Ramble

Laurel—Lewes—Greenwood—Laurel

Nestled between Chesapeake Bay tributaries and the Atlantic Ocean lies the gentle, scenic coastal plain of lower Delaware—terrain ideal for cycling at any level of experience. Although strong riders may want to make this flat ride through Delaware's rural Sussex County a one-day near-century challenge, it is best savored as it was designed: three days meandering leisurely from one luxurious bed-and-breakfast inn to the next.

Designed by cycling-enthusiast innkeepers Gwen North of Spring Garden Bed & Breakfast in Laurel and Betty Sharp and Cora Tennefoss in Greenwood, this ride takes the route offered as a self-guided package by their outfit, Biking Inn to Inn Delaware. (That hassle-free package—which is quite moderate in price—includes three nights in the inns for double occupancy, the transportation of your luggage from one inn to the next, three breakfasts and three dinners, snacks at each inn on arrival, detailed maps and cue sheets of side trips, parking for your car, and secure bicycle storage. For reservations or more information, call Ambassador Travel at 800–845–9939. Tell 'em you read it here.)

This trip, verified and updated by Bruce and Alfreda Clinton of Wilmington, Delaware, begins in Laurel (although beach-lovers may choose to start and end in Lewes). Once a thriving shipping center and port town, Laurel boasts more than 800 structures on the National Register of Historic Places. One of these is your starting point, Spring Garden Bed & Breakfast (302–875–7015), a restored eighteenth-century country manor furnished with eighteenth- and nineteenth-century antiques and fine art.

After a hearty breakfast you'll head for the beach town of Lewes (pronounced "Lewis")—the "First Town in the First State." The cycling is virtually flat, along agricultural backroads with little traffic. At Lewes, there are a growing number of bed-and-breakfast inns within half a mile of the Second Street business district (where, among other places for treats, you can visit the Lewes Bake Shoppe and King's Ice Cream—homemade!).

After a filling breakfast full of the complex carbohydrates that fuel a cyclist's legs, you'll head cross-country past farm lands and ponds and through historic Milton. One treat will be passing Colvine's Bison Farm—yes, buffalo in Delaware: On Route 16 just before your arrival at Greenwood, you are likely to see the out-of-place-looking creatures pasturing right on the side of the road. Just north of Greenwood is the Shawnee Inn (302–349–0878), a renovated family farm where you can sit and rock forever in the porch swing on the ample front and side porches, listening to the birds trill.

The return ride to Laurel includes passage on Delaware's last free cable ferry across a Chesapeake Bay tributary, the Nanticoke River, and a visit to the quaint shipbuilding village of Bethel, the only village in Delaware listed in its entirety on the National Register of Historic Places. Once again at Spring Garden B&B, you can retrieve your car and wave farewell to Gwen North as you head home.

The best times of year to take this ride are spring and fall, as it can "get bleeding hot" in the summer, with high humidity, remarks a local. You may want to pack some insect repellent as well.

The Basics

Start: Spring Garden Bed & Breakfast in Laurel, 0.2 mile west of Rte. 13 on Delaware Ave. Extended.

Length: 98.2 miles, divided into day-long segments of 34.5, 35.2, and 28.5 miles.

Terrain: Mostly flat. Traffic mostly light, except around the three towns.

Food: Occasional convenience stores en route, but carry some snacks and water. If you do this ride as part of the Biking Inn to Inn Delaware package, your breakfasts and dinners are included, and picnic lunches are available at an extra charge.

Miles & Directions

Note: Follow directions carefully, as not every small street is shown on the map.

First Day (Laurel to Lewes)

- 0.0   From the Spring Garden B&B parking lot, turn left onto Rd. 466 (Delaware Ave.).
- 0.3   Cross Rte. 13 and make an immediate right onto unmarked Rd. 465.
- 1.6   Bear left after passing Chipman's Pond and Old Christ Church on your left to stay on Rd. 465.
- 2.2   Turn left at the T intersection onto Rd. 74.
- 3.0   Take your first left turn after Rd. 74 onto unmarked Rd. 446. At about mile 8, cross Rte. 9 (Rd. 28) to continue on Rd. 446.
- 14.3 Turn left at the T intersection onto Rte. 9 (which is also County Rd. 28). In 0.4 mile, you'll pass a shopping center on the right. At mile 14.8, cross Rte. 113 and enter Georgetown.
- 15.4 Enter the traffic circle and turn right onto Rd. 431 (South Bedford St.). In 0.2 mile, Bodie's Dairy Market is on the left for drinks and snacks.

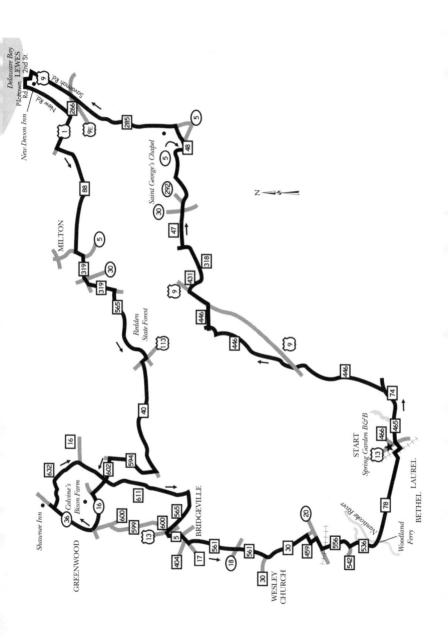

- 16.3 Turn left onto Rd. 318 (Park Ave.).
- 18.3 Turn right onto Rte. 47 (Springfield Rd.). At mile 20.5, Wilson's General Store is on your left at the stop sign at Rte. 30 (which is also County Rd. 248 and Gravel Hill Rd.).
- 24.3 Turn right at the T intersection onto Rte. 5.
- 24.9 Turn left at Rte. 48 (Holly Mt. Rd.) at sign to Christ Church. Indian Mission Church is on far left at this intersection and Wise Buys auto business is on the near right.
- 25.6 Turn left onto Rte. 23 (which is also County Rd. 285 and Beaver Dam Road). Christ Church is on the far left at this intersection.
- 31.5 At the stop sign that marks the end of Rte. 23, turn left and immediately right at the traffic light onto Rte. 9E. Follow Rte. 9E to the town of Lewes.
- 31.7 Cross Rte. 1 at the traffic light. Stay in the middle lane of this very busy intersection and proceed straight on Rte. 9. Continue to follow signs for Rte. 9E Business.
- 32.3 Bear left at the sign to Lewes.
- 34.4 Turn left onto 2nd Street 1 block before the traffic light. In 0.1 mile, Lewes Bake Shoppe is on the left and King's Ice Cream is 1 block farther on right. Bike around and enjoy this peaceful coastal community before arriving at your chosen bed-and-breakfast inn.

Second Day (Lewes to Greenwood)
- 0.0 From your chosen inn, proceed down 2nd St. Turn right at the T intersection onto Shipcarpenter St. and then turn left at the T intersection onto Pilottown Rd.
- 0.8 Turn left onto New Rd. (Rd. 266).
- 3.6 Turn right at the T intersection onto Rd. 266B (Massua Rd.).
- 3.9 At the yield sign merge onto the wide shoulder of the very busy Rte. 1N.
- 5.5 Turn left onto Rd. 88 (Cove Neck Rd.) at the sign to Milton.

- 11.4 At the stop sign turn left onto Rte. 5 (Federal St.). The Goshen Methodist Church is on the far right of this intersection. (*Note for a detour:* If you turn right or go straight at this intersection, you can visit the town of Milton, which has a number of lunch spots, like the Town Cafe or Norma's, 198 homes on the National Register of Historic Places, a lovely pond, and the mouth of the Broadkill River. King's Ice Cream is on Union St. on the left. Pick up snacks at Bodie's Dairy Market or the IGA. After your excursion return to this intersection to continue the main ride.)
- 11.9 Turn right onto Rd. 319 (Sand Hill Rd.) at the produce stand on your left.
- 15.0 Turn right onto Rd. 565 (E. Redden Rd.) at the sign for Ockels Farm Airport. At mile 16.4, Redden State Forest is a wonderful area for bird-watching. At mile 18.7 you'll pass a picnic area on your left.
- 19.2 Turn right onto the wide shoulder of busy Rte. 113 (Dupont Blvd.). Watch carefully for traffic! (Relax, you'll be on this road only 0.2 mile.)
- 19.4 Turn left onto Rd. 40 (Redden Rd.) at the signs for Bay Bridge and Bridgeville. At mile 21.5 you'll pass another picnic area on your left.
- 25.5 Make a sharp right turn onto Rd. 594 (Oak Rd.).
- 28.2 Turn left onto Rd. 602 soon after passing a sign for Hunters Cove Rd.
- 30.3 Turn left at the T intersection onto Rte. 16. At mile 30.8, Elmer's Market is on the right for fresh fruit and veggies. At mile 31.5, you should see the buffalo from Colvine's Bison Farm on your right.
- 32.4 Turn right onto the busy Rte. 36 (Shawnee Rd.) at the traffic light. Be careful, as there is only a narrow road shoulder on Rte. 36.
- 35.2 Turn left into the Shawnee Inn.

Third Day (Greenwood to Laurel)

- 0.0 Turn right out of Shawnee Inn onto Rte. 36. Watch for traffic!

- 0.9 Turn left onto Rd. 632 (Utica Rd.).

- 3.3 Bear right onto Rd. 611 (Judy Rd.). In 0.2 mile, cross Rte. 16 at a five-point intersection and continue straight on Owens Rd.

- 4.3 Bear left onto Sharps Mill Rd.

- 7.7 Turn right at the T intersection onto Rd. 565 (Sunnyside Rd.).

- 9.4 Turn left at the T intersection onto Rd. 600 (Fawn Rd.). At the stop sign at mile 10.1, be especially careful when crossing the four-lane Rte. 13.

- 10.3 Bear left at the stop sign onto Rd. 5 (Main St.). In 0.2 mile, Smith & Sons Fruit Market will be on your left. In the fall, the market features fresh-pressed apple cider.

- 10.9 Turn right at the traffic light onto Rte. 404W. (Note for a detour: If you go straight at this intersection, you may tour Bridgeville and visit the Rappa Brand Scrapple House.)

- 11.3 Continue straight at the traffic light onto Rte. 17. Do not follow Rte. 404, which heads right at this traffic light.

- 11.4 Turn left onto Rd. 561 (Wesley Church Rd.). Immediately, Delagra Corp. will be on your left.

- 15.7 Turn left at the T intersection onto Rd. 30 (Atlanta Rd.). Wesley Church is on the near right of this intersection.

- 18.5 Turn right at the traffic light onto Rte. 20 (Stein Highway). (Note for a detour: If you turn left or go straight at this intersection instead, you may tour Seaford and visit the John Ross Mansion and its Plantation.) In 0.1 mile, the Nylon Capitol Shopping Center is on the right, including a pizza parlor and Chinese restaurant. The pizza parlor has very clean rest rooms and the Chinese restaurant has the better facility for bicycle security (bikes can be viewed while eating at inside tables while the windows at the pizza parlor shield visibility).

- 19.2 Turn left onto Rd. 556 (Figgs Rd.).
- 20.2 Bear right at Craigs Pond onto Rd. 542A (Mill Rd.).
- 20.4 Turn left at the T intersection onto Rd. 542 (Butler Brand Rd.).
- 21.1 Bear right at the stop sign onto Rd. 536 (Woodland Rd.).
- 22.4 Turn left at the T intersection onto Rd. 78. In 0.2 mile, follow Rd. 78 as it turns left, and proceed to the Woodland Ferry. Take the ferry, which operates seven days a week (weather permitting) from sunrise to sunset at no charge, whenever its staff see people waiting to cross. Enjoy the two-minute ride across the Nanticoke River.
- 22.7 From the ferry dock, continue straight on Rd. 78 (Woodland Ferry Rd.). (Note for a detour: At mile 25.3, you may elect to turn right at the traffic light onto Rd. 493 and tour the town of Bethel.)
- 28.0 Cross Rte. 13A at the traffic light and bear left onto Rte. 9 (Georgetown Rd.).
- 28.2 Turn right onto Short Ave. at the end of the school field.
- 28.4 Turn left at the stop sign onto Delaware Ave.
- 28.5 Turn left into Spring Garden Bed & Breakfast. Welcome back!

4

CRABS Challenge

Delaware Seashore State Park—Fenwick Island—
Dagsboro—Millsboro—Rehoboth Beach—
Delaware Seashore State Park

Smell the salty air and feel the seashore breezes as the Come Ride Around the Bays of Sussex (CRABS) Challenge takes you on a scenic tour of the bays of Sussex County. This tour of the scenic inland estuaries of Delaware is the route featured by the CRABS organization in its fund-raising tour early each May, the entrance fee for which benefits the Delaware Inland Bays Estuary education program.

This ride will put you in contact with some of the state's most interesting wildlife as the bays form the northernmost portion of the pelican's annual middle-to-late-June Delaware migration. The bays are also home to wading birds, such as the egret and great blue heron. Sussex County is also in the north-south flyway for many species of song birds, some of which have flown all the way from South America to arrive at the same time horseshoe crabs are mating on Delaware's beaches. By feeding on the crab eggs, the birds double their body weight before crossing the Delaware Bay and continuing north.

In addition to the wildlife, this ride also offers many spots to take a cooling dip, including Holts Landing State Park on the Indian River (mile 24.5). The park offers picnic tables, a pavilion, a playground, a boat ramp, and a wading beach. Water at the park is drinkable, but sometimes has an odd color, odor, or taste—so don't refill your water bottle unless you are dying of thirst.

Another attraction is the museum of the Native American Naticokes, who still live in the Oak Orchard area (miles 39–45). For added fun, plan your trip for the weekend after Labor Day when the Naticokes host their large annual powwow.

And do your best to work up an appetite while riding or swimming as this route offers ample opportunities to chow down on the local delicacy of (appropriately enough) crab cakes. Among the best crab spots are Harpoon Hannah's and The Shark's Cove (at opposite ends of the bridge at mile 11.4), and Tom and Terry's on Route 54 (past mile 16.2). Later in the ride you can try more crab cakes at The Rusty Rudder (mile 58.0).

The ride, which is designed in 64- and 27-mile versions and varies from farmland to seashore, is largely flat but can be a challenge due to strong ocean winds, said route designer Larry Wonderlin of Rehoboth, Delaware. Despite the winds, the shorter version can be ridden by even the most casual of riders and the roads are very bicycle friendly. "I have twice cycled from Portland, Maine, to Orlando, Florida, with Pedal for Power, and I believe Delaware has the best cycling road on the East Coast," said Wonderlin. "Although we have been 'found,' traffic is still lower than in most places." Wonderlin added that even Delaware's busiest roads often offer wide, comfortable shoulders and the state's drivers remain, for the most part, bicycle friendly. "We're over 30 miles into this ride and no one has honked a horn," Wonderlin recalled one New Yorker commenting during a CRABS Challenge ride.

For those wishing to spread the ride over a copy of days, numerous bed-and-breakfast inns and motels are located in the towns through which you'll pass, including Rehoboth Beach, Dewey Beach, Bethany Beach, South Bethany, Fenwick Island, and Millsboro. For more information, call the Delaware Tourism Office at (800) 441–8846.

The Basics

Start: Delaware Seashore State Park Bath House parking lot just south of the Indian River Inlet Bridge on Rte. 1, on the ocean side of the road. The parking lot and beach are accessible year-round, although the bathhouse is open only from May 1 through September 30.

Length: 27 or 64 miles.

Terrain: Flat, although there can be strong winds requiring low gears in some sections. Traffic is generally moderately light to nonexistent, but in the few populated sections where it is heavy, the roads have wide paved shoulders.

Food: An assortment of fast-food places and restaurants are available from mile 4.0 to 16.0; the next available food is in the towns of Millville (mile 21.4), Dagsboro (mile 30.5), and Millsboro (mile 35) and at occasional convenience stores thereafter. Wonderlin's favorite lunch stop is Casapulla's at mile 52.7, where the steak sandwiches "rival South Philly steaks," and Ashby's Oyster House is "better than average" for seafood. Once on Route 1 again, Wonderlin notes, "you're in hog heaven."

Miles & Directions

Note: Follow directions carefully, as not every small street is shown on the map.

- 0.0 Turn right out of the parking lot and make a U-turn under the bridge.
- 0.3 Turn right onto Rte. 1S. At mile 4.8 continue straight at the intersection of Rte. 26. Mile 5 to 6 is a good time to stock up on food as this section of the ride includes the Bethany Bake Shop, Dunkin' Donuts and McDonalds.
- 10.8 Turn right at the traffic light onto Rtes. 20 and 54. The next 3 to 4 miles are busy with motor vehicles and a narrow road shoulder. Use caution.

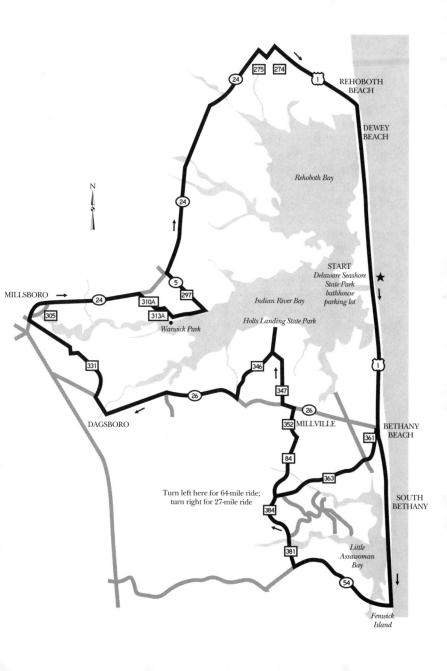

N

MILLSBORO →

RAHOBOTH BEACH

DEWEY BEACH

Rehoboth Bay

Indian River Bay

Holts Landing State Park

Warwick Park

DAGSBORO

MILLVILLE

START
Delaware Seashore
State Park
bathhouse
parking lot

BETHANY BEACH

SOUTH BETHANY

Turn left here for 64-mile ride;
turn right for 27-mile ride

Little
Assawoman
Bay

Fenwick
Island

- 14.6 Turn right onto unmarked Rd. 381, just before a Texaco service station and convenience store.
- 16.7 Bear right onto Rd. 384. In 0.5 mile you'll pass Lil Red School House—a nursery school that is indeed painted red. Decision time is approaching.
- 17.6 Bear left onto Rd. 84. Do not follow the sign to Camp Barnes unless you have decided to take the shorter route.

  For the shorter route, turn right instead onto Rte. 363 (sign reads TO CAMP BARNES*). At mile 18.9 bear right to stay on Rd. 363 (do not follow the second* CAMP BARNES *sign). At mile 21.0 turn right at the T intersection onto Rd. 361 (Kent Ave.) and ride over Little Assawoman Canal Bridge. At mile 22.4 turn right at the T intersection onto Rte. 26 (Garfield Pkwy.). At mile 22.5 turn left at the traffic light onto Rte. 1N. At mile 27.0 turn right into the parking lot alongside the bridge and re-enter Delaware Seashore State Park.*
- 17.9 Bear right to stay on Rd. 84.
- 19.9 Turn left onto unmarked Rd. 352 (Windmill Rd.).
- 21.0 Turn left at the stop sign onto Rte. 26 (Atlantic Ave.) in the village of Millville.
- 21.4 Turn right onto Rd. 347 (White Neck Rd.).
- 23.4 Bear left at the stop sign onto Rd. 346. (If you were to turn right instead, you would pass the entrance to Holts Landing State Park in about a mile.)
- 25.4 Turn right at the stop sign onto Rte. 26 (Atlantic Ave.).
- 30.5 In Dagsboro, turn right at the T intersection to stay on Rte. 26.
- 30.8 Go straight through the traffic light.
- 31.7 Turn right onto Rd. 331 (where the sign unfortunately reads for 336A, which intersects with Rd. 331 just after this turn), just across from the S&J Restaurant.
- 34.1 Bear left at the Y intersection to stay on Rd. 331.

- 35.1 You've now entered the town of Millsboro. To avoid waiting at the two traffic lights, turn right onto Morris St. and then turn left onto Dodd St.
- 35.3 Turn right onto Rte. 24 (Main St.).
- 39.4 Turn right onto unmarked Rd. 310A.
- 40.2 Turn left onto Rd. 313A as Rd. 310A dead-ends at the waterfront.
- 40.6 Turn right at the stop sign onto Rd. 313. In 0.5 mile you'll pass Warwick Park.
- 43.0 Turn left at the T intersection onto Rd. 297.
- 45.0 Turn right at the traffic light onto Rte. 24E (John J. Williams Hwy.). At mile 48.0 continue straight through the traffic light. At mile 50.6 Casapulla's in Peddler's Village on your left offers good steak sandwiches. At mile 53.2 cross over Love Creek Bridge.
- 53.6 Turn right at the traffic light onto Rd. 275.
- 54.3 Turn left at the stop sign onto Rd. 274.
- 54.6 Turn right onto Martins Rd.
- 55.1 Turn right onto Rte. 1S to Rehoboth Beach. The next 9 miles have heavy motor vehicle traffic, but the road has a wide, well-paved shoulder.
- 64.0 Turn right immediately after crossing Indian River Inlet Bridge. Re-enter Delaware Seashore State Park.

5

Sussex Ponds Cruise

Delmar—Portsville—Bethel—Trap Pond—Delmar

Aside from being ideal for cycling with its almost traffic-free and wooded backroads, Delaware's Sussex County has a fascinating ecology. Two of the ponds this ride passes—Trap Pond and Trussum Pond—represent the northernmost extent of the bald cypress trees growing out of the water in swamps for which the Deep South is famous. At Trussum Pond you may feel as though you're pedaling through a Louisiana bayou instead of in a corner of the Mid-Atlantic. Trap Pond is in a state park, which—in addition to views of the pond—offers picnic tables, rest rooms, drinking water, a camp store, and overnight camping during the summer (for more information call the Delaware Division of Parks in Dover: 302–736–4702.

This ride was devised and verified by Gilbert M. Turner of Salisbury, Maryland. The outbound route through flat, agricultural land will take you right through the place where the corner of Delaware juts into Maryland—the cornerstone there was the first laid by the surveyors Mason and Dixon in 1768. As the route passes through Portsville, unpack your binoculars for a bird-watching detour into the Nanticoke Wildlife Area.

The Basics

Start: Delmar, a town that straddles the border of Delaware and Maryland (and whose name obviously borrows from both states), in the parking lot for the strip mall in the Delaware half of the town; it is just north of Rte. 54 and just west of the southbound lane of Rte. 13. Park near Bonanza Restaurant at the south end of the parking lot.

Length: 42 miles.

Terrain: Flat. Traffic is light except on Rte. 54 and crossing Rte. 13.

Food: Many options at the start in Delmar; a country store just off the route in Bethel about 20 miles into the ride; and seasonal camp stores at Chipman Pond (mile 26) and at Trap Pond (mile 34). No other services in between, so carry snacks, water, and tools.

Miles & Directions

Note: Follow directions carefully, as not every small street is shown on the map.

- 0.0   Leaving the south end of the parking lot, turn right (west) onto Rte. 54 at the Delaware state line. At mile 6.5 continue straight to stay on Rte. 54 (don't follow curve to the right). At mile 7.8 you'll pass the cornerstone monument marking the Mason-Dixon Line and will now be riding briefly in Maryland.
- 8.7   Turn right onto Norris Twilley Rd.
- 9.3   Bear right onto May Twilley Rd. In about 0.75 mile you'll re-enter Delaware, where the road you're on becomes Rd. 507.
- 11.2 Immediately after crossing Rd. 76, turn right onto Rd. 508.
- 12.7 Where Rd. 508 jogs right to continue straight, turn left onto Rd. 509.
- 14.8 Turn left onto Rd. 514.
- 15.8 Cross Rte. 24 and continue straight on Rd. 493 into Portsville. (To detour into the Nanticoke Wildlife Area, at Portsville turn left onto Rd. 496 and ride to the end; return the way you came in.) At Portsville continue on Rd. 493, which bends east past the pond and takes you into Bethel at mile 19.8. Cross the bridge and pass a country store on Main St. to your left. Continue on Rd. 493.

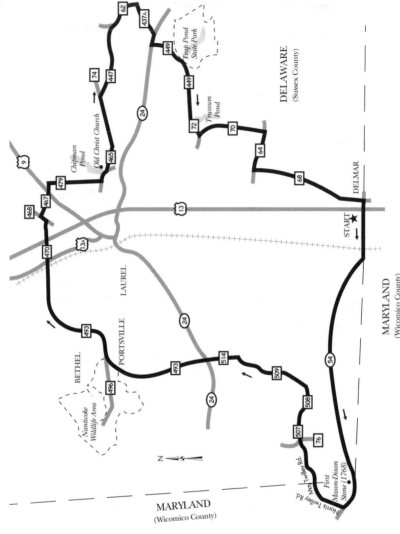

DELAWARE
(Sussex County)

MARYLAND
(Wicomico County)

MARYLAND
(Wicomico County)

Trap Pond
State Park

Trussum
Pond

Chipman
Pond

Old Christ Church

DELMAR

START

LAUREL

PORTSVILLE

BETHEL

Nanticoke
Wildlife Area

First
Mason-Dixon
Stone (1768)

Norris Twilley Rd.

N

- 22.4 Cross Rte. 13A and continue straight on Rd. 470.
- 23.0 Cross Rd. 13 and continue straight on Rd. 470 until the end.
- 23.7 Turn left at the T intersection onto Rd. 468.
- 23.8 Turn right onto Rd. 467. In 0.7 mile you'll cross US Rte. 9/Rte. 28.
- 24.7 Turn right onto Rd. 479.
- 26.2 Turn left onto Rd. 465. Just after this corner is a camp store, where you can provision up if you're hungry or thirsty. In 500 feet cross over Chipman Pond Dam. Less than 0.25 mile later is Old Christ Church on your left, an early-eighteenth-century "chapel of ease," where the interior—including the pews—is still original, unpainted wood. By the way, for the next 5 miles you'll be riding on the first 5 miles of Ride 3.
- 27.2 Bear left to join Rd. 74.
- 28.5 Turn right onto Rd. 447.
- 30.7 Bear right to join Rd. 62.
- 31.5 Turn right onto Rd. 437A.
- 32.5 Turn right at the T intersection onto Rte. 24.
- 32.7 Turn left onto Rd. 449 at the sign to Trap Pond State Park. At mile 33.9 is the entrance to the park itself. South of the park Rd. 449 bends right (west). At mile 35.5 cross over the dam for Trussum Pond, which lies to your left and is very pretty with its stand of bald cypress trees.
- 35.7 Continue straight on Rd. 72.
- 36.0 Turn sharply left at the stop sign onto Rd. 70 where Rd. 72 curves right. Go slowly here, for this intersection is easy to miss.
- 37.9 Turn right at the T intersection onto Rd. 64.
- 38.9 Turn left onto Rd. 68.
- 42.1 Turn right onto Rte. 54/Rd. 419.
- 42.2 Cross Rte. 13 at the traffic light. Turn right into the mall parking area.

6

Amish Country Challenge

Dover—Hartly—Marydel—Felton—
Camden—Wyoming— Dover

Like many rural routes, this ride will take you past picturesque farms, green meadows, and quaint old buildings. But unlike other rides, the route will also take you past slow-moving horse-drawn buggies and traditional Amish women tending their gardens. The Amish Country Challenge follows lightly traveled backroads from the historic town and state capital of Dover into outlying farmland and through the heart of central Delaware's Amish country.

The Amish, originally from Switzerland, follow the Mennonite religion, which was formed around 1536 when Catholic priest Menno Simons broke from the church. The Amish first settled in the area in 1757 after heading south to avoid spreading into the territory of the French and Indian War. Like other Amish settlements, the Delaware Amish adapted to the local agriculture and have been steady providers of the area's corn and soybean crops.

Along this ride you'll see many of the traditional Amish sights, including the horse and buggy, dark clothing, and simple farm structures without electricity. However, some of the group have taken on more modern ways and will occasionally accept an automobile ride into town and other modern conveniences.

Despite this route's 62-mile length, it can be easily completed in an afternoon. It is extremely flat and follows lightly traveled roads—many of which have ample shoulders. The route is also dotted with small farming towns, such as Felton and Marydel, where riders can rest and grab a bite to eat.

The challenge begins in the heart of Dover's downtown district, which includes the Old Stat House circa 1792, Constitution Park, and the legislative hall where Delaware's General Assembly now meets. For more information about the area call the Tourism Bureau of Kent County at (302) 734–4888.

This ride, which is also an annual supported tour and charity event benefiting the Brain Injury Association of Delaware, was submitted and verified by Karen and Tom Hartley of Dover. For more information about participating in the official tour, call (302) 697–6400.

The Basics

Start: Delaware Visitors Center, Dover, DE, (302) 739–4266. From Baltimore, MD., take Hwy. 50/301 through Annapolis, MD, and across the Chesapeake Bay Bridge. After the bridge, continue north on Hwy. 301 to Maryland Rte. 302. Turn right onto Rte. 302 and follow to Templeville, where you will turn right onto Rte. 454. Rte. 454 will become Rte. 8 in Delaware. Follow Rte. 8 east into Dover. Bear right at a fork in the road onto Loockerman St. and follow to Federal St. Turn right onto Federal. The Visitors Center will be on your right. From Philadelphia, PA, take I–95S through Wilmington, DE, where you will pick up Rte. 1S. Follow Rte. 1S to exit 104 (Historic Dover and Convention Center). Turn left after exiting onto Rte. 13, which you will follow to Loockerman St. Turn right onto Loockerman and then left onto Federal St. The Visitors Center will be just ahead.

Length: 61.51 miles.

Terrain: Extremely flat with plenty of places to rest. This is a good route for someone ready to try a little longer ride, but not quite ready for a century.

Food: This is a mostly rural ride with few stores along the way. However, water and snacks can be found at the beginning of the ride in Dover and in Marydel (mile 20) and Woodside (mile 55).

Miles & Directions

- 0.0   Turn right onto Federal St. out of the Delaware Visitors Center.
- .08   Turn right onto Water St.
- 0.3   Turn right onto N. State St.
- 1.3   Turn left onto Walker Rd.
- 2.2   Continue straight on Walker Rd.
- 3.1   Turn right onto Chestnut Grove Rd.
- 4.9   Turn right onto Madistone Branch Rd.
- 5.4   Turn left onto W. Denney's Rd.
- 6.4   Turn right onto Blue Heron Rd.
- 7.1   Turn left onto Pearson's Corner Rd.
- 8.1   Turn right onto Dinah's Corner Rd.
- 9.7   Turn left onto Judith Rd.
- 10.9   Turn right onto Lockwood Chapel Rd.
- 12.7   Continue straight onto Ford's Corner Rd.
- 14.7   Continue Straight onto Butterpat Rd.
- 17.5   Continue straight onto Hourglass Rd.
- 17.9   Turn right onto Taralia Rd.
  Note: A small food store is located here in the town of Marydel.
- 20.6   Turn left onto Strauss Rd.
- 20.6   Turn right onto Firehouse Ln.
- 20.8   Turn left onto Rte. 8, then right onto Maryland Rd. 311.
- 22.0   Turn left onto Bee Tree Rd.
- 22.3   Continue straight onto Westville Rd.
- 29.5   Turn left onto Hazlettville Rd.
- 31.0   Turn left onto Nault Rd.
- 31.9   Turn right onto Yoder Dr.
- 33.1   Turn right onto Rose Valley School Rd.
- 33.8   Turn left onto Hazlettville Rd.
- 34.8   Turn left onto Apple Grove School Rd.

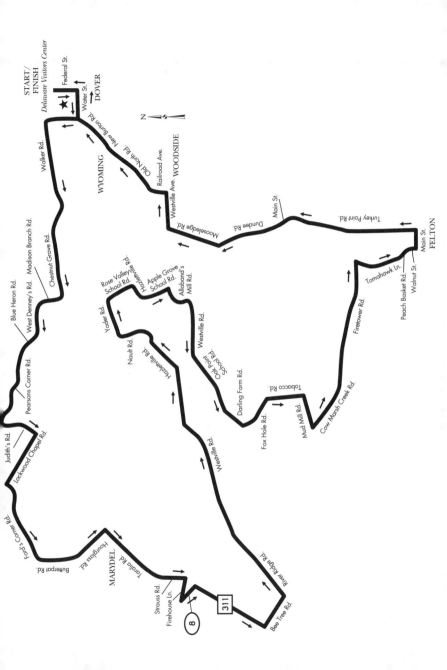

- 35.4 Turn right onto Allaband's Mill Rd.
- 35.8 Turn right onto Westville Rd.
- 37.8 Turn left onto Oak Point School Rd.
- 38.8 Turn left onto Darling Farm Rd.
- 39.9 Turn left onto Fox Hole Rd.
- 40.8 Turn right onto Tobacco Rd.
- 41.8 Turn right onto Mud Mill Rd.
- 42.5 Turn left onto Cow Marsh Creek Rd.
- 44.0 Continue straight onto Firetower Rd.
- 47.5 Turn right onto Tomahawk Ln.
- 48.7 Turn left onto Peach Basket Rd.
- 49.2 Turn right onto Walnut St.
- 49.9 Turn left onto Main St., Felton.
- 50.0 Turn left onto Turkey Point Rd.
- 54.5 Turn left onto Main St.
- 54.7 Turn right onto Dundee/Mooseledge Rd.
  Note: A second small grocery store is located here.
- 54.7 Turn right onto Westville Rd.
- 55.4 Turn left onto Railroad Ave.
- 55.7 Turn right onto Old North Rd.
- 56.4 Turn left onto New Burton Rd.
- 58.3 Turn right onto Water St.
- 61.0 Turn left onto Federal St.
- 61.5 Arrive back at the Delaware Visitors Center.

7

Southern Delaware
Heritage Challenge

Bridgeville—Seaford—Bethel—Laurel—Millsboro—
Milton—Milford—Greenwood—Bridgeville

Few activities, cycling or otherwise, showcase the people, places, and culture of southern Delaware as comprehensively and enjoyably as the Southern Delaware Heritage Trail. The flat, easy, 106-mile ride takes you by the area's ponds, over its rivers, through its small towns and into its neighborhoods. The route follows a meandering loop linking southern Delaware's most historic towns—each with its own unique character.

The ride begins in the tiny town of Bridgeville, which is home to the T. S. Smith Apple Orchard and Produce Market—one of the largest of its kind in the state. Leaving Bridgeville, on the outskirts of the town of Seaford, you'll pass the UNOI Grain Mill (formerly known as the Hearn and Rawlins Mill). The restored, century-old mill (302) 629–4083 continues to use traditional stone grinding methods and is working to restore the waterwheel on its picturesque dam. Passing the mill, you'll cross into Maryland before returning to Seaford and a ride on the Woodland Ferry (www.woodlandferry.com), one of the last cable-run ferries in the United States. You'll then pedal into the old shipbuilding village of Bethel, where the entire town is listed on the National

Register of Historic Places. Next in line is the town of Laurel, home to the nature trails, meandering waterways, and bird watching of the Trap Pond State Park (302–875–5153). Like Bethel, Laurel also features many historic homes and has the largest historic district in the state. A few miles later you'll again straddle the Delaware/Maryland line before heading north to the American Indian history of Millsboro.

The Millsboro area was home to the Delaware Nanticoke Indian Tribe and now honors the culture with the Nanticoke Indian Museum and an annual two-day powwow each September. The museum is off the main bicycle route, so call the museum at (304) 945–7022 for directions.

The Heritage Challenge continues north into the town of Milton, which has been the home of five former Delaware governors. The unusally high gubernatorial residency is noted with the graceful Governor's Walk nestled between the Broadkill River and Wagamon's Pond. Milton also features numerous waterways and wildlife areas.

The last 20 miles passes the graceful architecture and restored bed and breakfasts of Milford and the tiny town of Greenwood on the route back to Bridgeville. Just a few of the many attractions in these historic towns are mentioned in this chapter. Each community offers hidden treasures—such a 225-year-old church in Laurel, a shipbuilding museum in Milford, and a canoe trail in Milton—for those willing to spend a little extra time exploring.

Phone numbers for information concerning each town's attractions are listed below.

Though this route is often completed in a day, lodging is available in most towns for those preferring to explore or who need a few breaks to complete this long, but pleasant century ride.

For more information call the Laurel Chamber of Commerce (302) 875–9319, the Greater Seaford Chamber of Commerce (302) 875–9319, the Greater Millsboro Chamber of Commerce

(302) 934–6777, the Milton Chamber of Commerce (302) 684–1101, or the Greater Milford Chamber of Commerce at (302) 422–3344.

The Heritage Trail was designed through a private-public partnership between local businesses and the Southern Delaware Tourism Bureau. The interpretation presented in this book is based on information provided by Sussex County cyclist and advocate Bill Davis and Delaware Bicycle and Pedestrian Coordinator Elizabeth Holloway.

The Basics

Start: RAPA Brand Scrapple Factory, Rte. 18, Bridgeville, DE. From Washington, D.C., take Hwy. 50E to Rte. 404E. Follow Rte. 404 to the RAPA factory in Bridgeville. From Dover, DE., follow Rte. 13S into Bridgeville. Bear right onto Rte. 13A. Turn right onto Market Skeet and follow to the factory.

Length: 115.8 miles.

Terrain: Though long, the Heritage Challenge is an extremely easy and pleasant ride with almost no climbs and plenty of places to stop, rest, and eat.

Food: Restaurants, grocery stores, and lodging are available every 10 to 15 miles in the route's larger towns. Shops and delis between the larger towns are noted in the "Miles & Directions" section.

Miles & Directions

- 0.0   Turn left out of the RAPA Brand Scrapple Factory onto Rte. 18.
- 0.64 Turn left onto Wesley Church Rd. (Rd. 561).
- 3.2   Turn left at the flashing traffic light back onto Rte. 18 and continue across the railroad tracks.

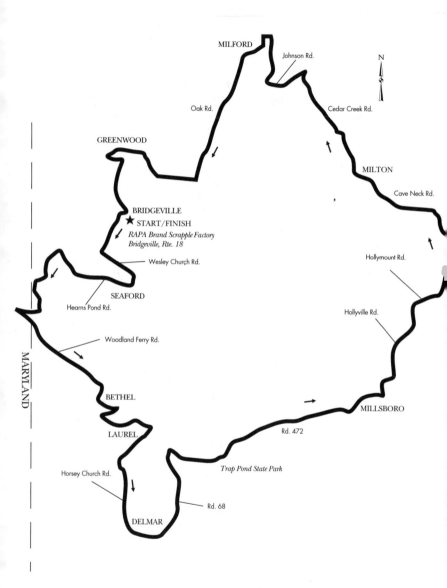

MILFORD

Johnson Rd.

N

Oak Rd.

Cedar Creek Rd.

GREENWOOD

MILTON

Cave Neck Rd.

BRIDGEVILLE

★ START/FINISH

RAPA Brand Scrapple Factory
Bridgeville, Rte. 18

Wesley Church Rd.

Hollymount Rd.

SEAFORD

Hearns Pond Rd.

Hollyville Rd.

Woodland Ferry Rd.

MARYLAND

BETHEL

Millsboro

LAUREL

Rd. 472

Trap Pond State Park

Horsey Church Rd.

Rd. 68

DELMAR

- 4.7   Bear right onto Elks Rd.(Rd. 46).

  Note: You are on the outskirts of the town of Seaford, which, in addition to the mill and ferry listed below, offers numerous historic and natural attractions, such as the Nanticoke River and the Seaford Historical Museum (302) 628–9828. For more information about Seaford call the Greater Seaford Chamber of Commerce (302) 629–9690.

- 5.7   Turn right onto Hearns Mill Rd. (Rte. 13A). This road looks a bit busy, but has a nice, wide shoulder.

- 6.1   Turn right onto Hearns Pond Rd. (Rd. 544).

  Note: The UNOI Mill is a nice place to stop and check out the scenery. You can walk your bike to the mill's working dam, buy some flour, or simply check out this century-old, stone-ground flour mill.

- 8.2   Turn right onto Atlanta Rd. (Rd.30).

- 11.5   Turn left onto Rte. 18 in the village of Atlanta.

- 12.4   Turn left onto Callaway Rd. (Rd. 558).

- 13.8   Turn right onto Neal's School House Rd. (Rd.553).

- 14.4   Turn left onto N. Oak Grove Rd. (Rd. 549). The church to your right is in Delaware and the church graveyard is in Maryland.

  Note: Keep your eyes open for a 200-year-old stone marker on the right noting the Mason Dixon line.

- 16.0   Turn right immediately after the railroad tracks onto Willin Rd. (Rd. 549B).

- 16.2   Turn left onto Woodland Ferry Rd. (Rd. 577), which has a wide shoulder. Follow Rd. 577 into the village of Reliance. The town has a small market where you can stock up on snacks and drinks.

- 17.2   Turn left onto Delaware Rte. 20. The market will be across the street. You are on the Maryland/Delaware state line.

- 17.2   Turn right onto Woodland Ferry Rd. (Rd. 78). A church will be at this intersection.

- 21.4 Take the short Woodland Ferry ride across the Nanticoke River.

  Note: A park with benches, shade trees, and a water view near the ferry is a nice place to rest while waiting to cross.

- 21.4 Continue straight on Rte. 78 after the ferry ride.

- 22.4 Take your first right turn onto Rd. 487A. (Beagle Club Rd.). Follow Rd. 487A until it dead ends at a T intersection in the town of Bethel.

  Note: Bethel is an interesting, old shipbuilding town in which every house is listed on the National Register. It's a pleasant place to stop and walk around. It also offers a sub shop and small market for those who have worked up an appetite.

- 23.0 Turn left at the T intersection in Bethel onto an un-marked road.

- 23.0+Turn almost immediately right across the bridge onto Bethel Rd. (Rd. 493). At low tide you can see the remnants of the original docks.

- 23.5 Turn left at the pond onto Rd. 492 (Portsville Rd.) to-ward Laurel.

- 26.4 In Laurel, bear left onto Rte. 24, then turn left onto Horsey Church Rd., where you will find food and snacks.

  Note: This ride is designed as a challenging one-day route; however, if you would like to stretch the trip with a stay in Laurel try the Spring Garden Bed and Breakfast on Delaware Ave. (302) 875–7015. For more information call the Laurel Chamber of Commerce at (302) 875–9319.

- 38.3 Turn left at the traffic light in Delmar onto State Line Rd. (Rte. 54).

- 42.3 Cross Rte. 13 and turn left onto Rd. 68.

- 50.6 Turn right onto Gordy Rd. (Rd. 70.).

- 52.6 Turn left onto Rd. 72.

- 52.7 Bear left onto Rd. 449, which leads to Trap Pond State Park (302) 875–5153. Bathrooms are available here.

- 54.7 Turn right onto Rte. 24.
- 54.7+ Turn left onto Rd. 437A.
- 55.5 Turn left onto Rd. 62 and then right onto Rd. 472.
- 60.6 Turn left onto Rte. 24 toward Millsboro.
- 63.5 Enter the town of Millsboro and turn right onto Betts Pond Rd. You'll then turn left onto the John J. Williams Hwy., and left again onto Hollyville Rd. (Rd. 305).
  Note: You're roughly halfway through the ride with 50.61 miles remaining to Bridgeville. If you have the stamina, go for it. If not, the Atlantic Budget Inn (302) 934–6711 on Rte. 113 is a good place to rest up for tomorrow's finish. For more Millsboro information call the Greater Millsboro Chamber of Commerce (302) 934–6777.
- 67.8 Continue straight on Hollymount Rd.
- 68.5 Turn left onto Beaver Dam Rd.
- 72.0 Turn left onto Dairy Farm Rd.
- 73.3 Continue straight onto Sweetbriar Rd.
- 74.0 Enter the town of Milton and turn left onto Cave Neck Rd.
- 77.3 Turn right onto Front St.
- 77.9 Continue straight on Union St.
- 78.8 Turn left onto Cedar Creek Rd.
- 86.2 Enter Milford and turn left onto Johnson Rd.
  Note: You are almost finished, with a mere 27.93 miles to go. However, if you can't pedal another inch, spend the evening at the nearby Towers/Banking House Inn and Restaurant (302) 422–3814 on Front St. For more information call the Milton Chamber of Commerce at (302) 684–1101.
- 88.9 Turn right onto Marshall St. (Rd. 225).
- 91.6 Turn left onto Second St. (Rd. 95).
- 92.0 Turn left onto Walnut St. (Rd. 213).
- 92.5 Turn right onto Seabury Ave.
- 92.8 Seabury Ave. will become Shawnee Rd.
- 95.3 Turn left onto N. Union Church Rd.

- 97.7 Turn right onto Oak Rd.
- 104.5 Turn right onto Tuckers Rd.
- 107.1 Turn right onto St. Johnstown Rd. (Rte. 16).
  Note: Use caution as you cross upcoming Rte. 13. As you cross, you will pass two traffic lights within roughly 100 yards.
- 109.3 Enter the town of Greenwood and turn left onto Market St.
- 110.1 Bear left after the flashing traffic light onto Hickman Rd. (Rte. 32).
- 110.6 Turn left onto Mile Stretch Rd. (Rte. 590).
- 111.8 Turn right at the stop sign onto Cocked Hat Rd. (Rd. 583).
- 114.7 Cross the Rte. 404 Bypass. To cross the bypass you will have to turn right onto Rte. 404 for about 30 yards before crossing over to continue on Rd. 583. Follow Rd. 583 back into Bridgeville.
- 115.7 Enter Bridgeville and turn right at a T intersection onto Rte. 13A. On your left is the T. S. Smith Orchard and Produce Market.
- 115.8 Turn right onto Market Street and follow back to the RAPA Brand Scrapple Factory.

Maryland

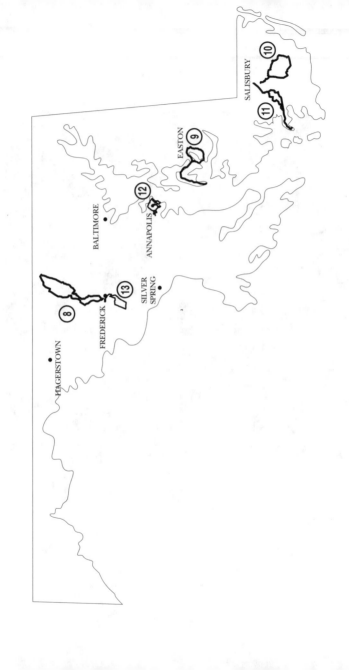

SALISBURY

⑩

⑪

EASTON

⑨

BALTIMORE

•

⑫

ANNAPOLIS

SILVER
SPRING

•

⑬

⑧

FREDERICK

HAGERSTOWN

•

Maryland

8

Three Covered Bridges Cruise

Frederick—Motters—Thurmont—Catoctin—Frederick

Be sure to pack your camera for this 44-mile jaunt into the northern part of Frederick County. Rolling, lightly traveled roads take you through a valley from which you can gaze at the distant Blue Ridge Mountains. At the northernmost section look for the imposing shrine of Mount Saint Mary's College in the mountains.

Besides the three nineteenth-century covered bridges through which you will ride, you might want to spend some time at the Catoctin Wildlife Preserve (301–271–3180) or www.zwpzoo.com, one of two privately owned zoos in Maryland. And don't miss the chance to poke around the ruins of an old lime kiln in the historic Catoctin Furnace area; the kiln dates back to the late 1700s. South of Thurmont you'll ride past various fish hatchery ponds.

This ride, one of a series produced by the Tourism Council of Frederick County, Inc., along with the Frederick-based bicycle shop Wheel Base, Inc., and verified by John Fiesler of the Tourism Council of Frederick County, Inc., is especially nice on a spring day when the orchards are fragrant with flowers, or in the autumn when their boughs are heavy with apples. Leave some space in your panniers to stash a few of each!

For those wishing to break up the 44-mile cruise into an easier two-day jaunt, there are several overnight options in Thurmont,

26 miles into the ride. Campers may set up a tent at Catoctin Mountain Park (301–663–9330) or at Crow's Nest Campground (301–271–7632). Those preferring luxury can rent a secluded cabin at Ole Mink Farm (301–271–7012) or relax with a free continental breakfast at the quaint Cozy Country Inn (301–271–4301). Staying at Thurmont then makes the second day's return to Frederick a mere 17 miles.

Frederick also has several bed-and-breakfast inns. Particularly notable is the Tyler-Spite House (301–831–4455), an elegantly restored three-story 1814 Federal-style mansion, where your stay includes afternoon tea. For information on other choices, contact the Tourism Council of Frederick County at (800) 999–3613.

The Basics

Start: Frederick at Culler Lake, at the corner of W. 2nd St. and College Terrace. Free parking is available on the street. Rest rooms are open near the tennis courts from noon to 8 P.M. Labor Day through Memorial Day. To get to the start from I–70 or I–270, take Rte. 15 north to the Rosemont Ave. exit. Go straight at the light onto 2nd St. Culler Lake will be on your right. Park along 2nd St.

Length: 44 miles.

Terrain: Moderately rolling hills. Traffic generally light but heavier around Frederick. Note: Verifier Marks led the successful campaign to get Maryland traffic law changed to allow bicyclists to use the shoulders of most non-freeway controlled-access highways, such as Rte. 15.

Food: Readily available in Frederick and Thurmont, with convenience stores scattered along the rest of the route. To be on the safe side, carry snacks and water.

Miles & Directions

- 0.0 Head west on W. 2nd St. The lake should be on your left.
- 0.2 Turn right onto Fairview Ave.

- 1.3 Turn left onto Motter Ave.; after crossing Rte. 15 a mile or 2 later, the name changes to Opossumtown Pike. At about mile 4, at McClellan Rd. and the Willowbrook Housing Development, bear left to stay on Opossumtown Pike.
- 5.5 Turn right (at Ford Rd.) to stay on Opossumtown Pike.
- 6.1 Bear left at the bottom of the hill to stay on Opossumtown Pike.
- 6.2 Turn right onto Masser Rd.
- 8.0 Turn right onto Mountaindale Rd.
- 8.2 Turn left onto Hansonville Rd.
- 8.4 Cross Rte. 15 and turn left onto unmarked Rte. 806, here called Hessong Bridge Rd.
- 9.5 Turn right onto Utica Rd. Here you'll pass through the first of the three covered bridges, Utica Mills Covered Bridge, built about 1850.
- 10.7 Turn left at the T intersection onto Old Frederick Rd.
- 14.7 Bear left at the stop sign onto Rte. 550 (Creagerstown Rd.).
- 15.0 Turn right onto the continuation of Old Frederick Rd. At mile 17.1 you'll pass through the Loys Station Covered Bridge, also built around 1850. If you're so inclined, stop to have a snack at the picnic tables at Loys Station Park or to use the rest rooms there.
- 21.0 Turn left at the stop sign onto unmarked Rte. 76 (Motters Station Rd.)
- 21.6 Turn left onto Old Kiln Rd. Soon you'll pass the old lime kiln on your right. Watch for gravel on the road.
- 24.1 Turn left at the T intersection onto unmarked Roddy Rd. At mile 25.7 you'll pass through the third of the covered bridges, Roddy Covered Bridge, built about 1856. Keep going straight where the road becomes Apples Church Rd., in the village of Thurmont.

N

76
Motters Station Rd.
MOTTERS
Old Kiln Rd.

Roddy Covered Bridge

15
E. Main St.
Roddy Rd.
Apples Church Rd.
THURMONT
Motter St.

Old Frederick Rd.

Frederick Rd.

77
Loys Station Park
covered bridge

806
Catoctin Mountain Zoological Park

550
Creagerstown Rd.
CREAGERSTOWN

Catoctin Furnace

Auburn Rd.

Fish Hatchery Rd.
Hessong Bridge Rd.
Utica Rd.
Old Frederick Rd.

UTICA
Utica Mills Covered Bridge

Bethel Rd.

Masser Rd.
Hansonville Rd.

Ford Rd.

15

Opossumtown Pike

Yellow Springs Rd.

Rosemont Ave.
Motter Ave.

40
15
W. 2d St.
Fairview Ave.
FREDERICK
★ START

- 26.8 Turn right at the T intersection onto Rte. 77 (E. Main St.).

- 27.5 Turn left onto Rte. 806 (Water St.). (*Note for a detour:* Continue west on Rte. 77 a bit more than 3 miles, past Catoctin Visitors Center, to Conningham Falls Trail on the left. It's only a quarter of a mile to the falls on this level, wheelchair-accessible trail. Return to the main ride by retracing your route downhill on Rte. 77, which is narrow and winding, with weekend traffic.)

- 27.6 Turn right to stay on Rte. 806, which is now called Frederick Rd. Several miles ahead the Catoctin Mountain Zoological Park will be on your left. Stay on Rte. 806 as it crosses Rte. 15, changing its name to Auburn Rd. (no sign). Be careful at that crossing, as traffic is fast and heavy.

- 33.4 Turn right onto the wide, smooth shoulder of busy Rte. 15.

- 34.1 Turn left onto Fish Hatchery Rd. Now you will pass fish ponds.

- 34.7 Turn left onto Bethel Rd.

- 39.4 Turn left onto Yellow Springs Rd. at the stop sign. In Frederick this road becomes Rosemont Ave. Watch for dangerous grates and traffic.

- 44.0 Turn right onto W. 2nd St.

9

Farmer's and Fisherman's Ramble

Easton—Oxford—St. Michael—Easton

For more than 300 years farmers have plowed the thin strips of land and fishermen have navigated the narrow channels of water slicing though this isolated section of Maryland's Eastern Shore. And as you pedal this slow-paced, family-friendly ride, you'll see that those industries have been preserved over the centuries and continue to shape the modern character of these small communities.

The ride begins in the town of Easton, which was founded in 1708 and was once in the running to serve as an alternative state capital to Annapolis. Though it never came to be, the town was to serve as "Capital of the Eastern Shore," said one local historian. As you ride out of Easton along wide, winding county roads, you will pass the town's many working farms where corn, soybeans, and wheat remain the dominant crops. The town also remains one of the country's largest Quaker gathering places.

After passing the overhead stalks of the cornfields and small roadside produce stands, you'll arrive in the town of Oxford, which being a bit closer to the Chesapeake Bay served for many years as the area's major port town. Though the scenic village has become largely residential with most of the boats being of the leisure cruise variety, a few fisherman continue to ply their trade from the Oxford pier. The ride takes you to the pier where a seaside eatery (Pier Street Restaurant 410–226–5171) provides a long-range view of the fishermen as they begin and end their day on the water. Just a little farther down the road, you'll also want to stop in on locals Myrtle "Mert" Bringman and her son Bill. Together they have been running the little convenience store, better known as the Tred Avon Confectionery, for four decades and proudly claim their store as the longest running business in town. Mert's made the same sandwiches every morning for 41 years, she'll proudly tell you.

After chatting with the Bringmans (and downing an ice cream cone or two), you'll cross the Tred Avon River aboard the nation's oldest—according to a historical marker—privately owned ferry service. Ten-minute crossings aboard the Oxford Bellevue Ferry began in 1683 and have operated continuously since 1836.

The ferry ride is followed once more by a rural, winding ride into the popular and historic town of St. Michaels. The town, now home to a picturesque harbor and dozens of period-style antique shops, restaurants, and waterfront inns, was settled in 1677 by shipbuilders and tobacco farmers.

The Chesapeake Bay Maritime Museum, one of the town's main attractions and a place where visitors can easy spend an afternoon, preserves the seaside traditions with ongoing boat restoration projects, the nation's largest collection of Chesapeake Bay watercraft, and a museum explaining the history of the bay. The museum also features a 120-year-old lighthouse and a wharf where visitors can try their hand at catching blue crabs or tonging for oysters before heading back to Easton.

This ride is excellent for casual cyclists as it is relatively short, almost entirely flat, and with most roads accompanied by wide shoulders. It is a popular route for the Freestate Derailleurs Bicycle Club, said club member and Baltimore resident Frank Pondolfina, who submitted the information on which the ride is based.

At a little less than 30 miles, the route is designed to be completed in an afternoon. However, if you would like to spend an evening call the St. Michaels Business Association at (800) 660–9471 or the Talbot County Chamber of Commerce at (410) 822–4653 for lodging information.

An optional ride of 60.4 miles along a windy and a little more challenging section down to Tilghman Island is also included in the Miles & Directions section.

The Basics

Start: Tred Avon Square shopping center parking lot, Rte. 322, Easton, MD. From Washington, D.C., take U.S. 50 over the Chesapeake Bay Bridge and continue for 25 miles. Take Rte. 322 toward Oxford. Turn left at Marlboro Rd. and into Tred Avon Square. From the south, take U.S. 50 West to Rte. 322 toward Oxford. Turn left into shopping center.

Length: 29.2 miles (An additional 31.2-mile option is also included in the "Miles & Directions" section for a total ride of 60.4 miles.)

Terrain: Though some might find a 30-mile ride intimidating, this is one of the easiest routes in the book. The route is almost completely flat with wide riding shoulders and plenty of spots to rest and recover along the way.

Food: Stock up on supplies at the start because no food or drink is available the first 10 miles. You'll find a restaurant at mile 11. General stores and rest rooms are scattered every couple of miles during the ride's middle section. Remember to stock up before returning from St. Michaels as the last 10 miles are also without amenities.

Miles & Directions

- 0.0   Turn left at the traffic light out of Tred Avon Square shopping center onto Rte. 322. It's a busy road but has a nice wide shoulder.
- 0.3   Pass through first traffic light

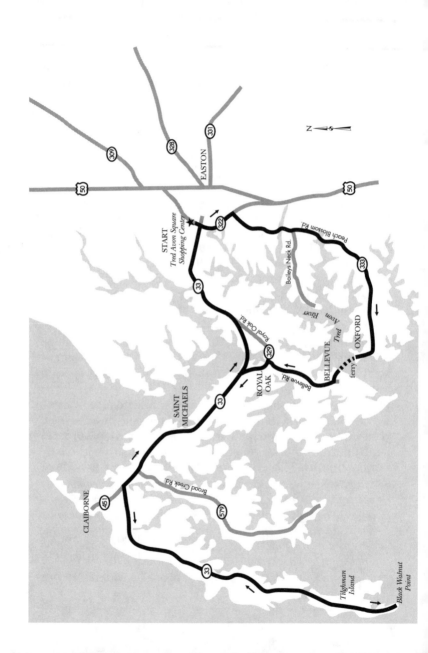

- 1.2   Pass second traffic light.
- 1.8   Turn right at your third traffic light onto Oxford Road (Scenic Rte. 333). You can now settle in for a pleasant ride along a lightly traveled rural road with a wide shoulder.
- 3.2   You'll pass a smalltown "Christmas Shop."
- 3.7   Cross Peach Blossom Creek.
- 5.2   Cross Trippe Creek.
- 7.4   You'll pass Eason's produce stand on your left.
- 10.1   On your right, will be Oxford's Spirits, Beer and Deli.
- 10.5   You'll reach the town of Oxford with the Tred Avon River and marina on your right.
- 10.5   Turn left onto South Morris St.
- 10.7   Turn right onto West Pier St.

    Note: You'll arrive at the Pier Street Restaurant (410) 226–5171 with a big red crab on the sign. You are about one-third of the way through the ride so feel free to stop for lunch. The restaurant, with its open wrap-around deck over the river, is open April 1st through Thanksgiving.

- 11.0   Leave the restaurant and head back out West Pier St.
- 11.2   Turn left back onto South Morris St. past the park on your right.
- 11.4   Bear left at the fork to continue on Bellevue Road.
- 11.6   The Tred Avon Confectionery (convenience store) will be on your right. To reach the Oxford Museum (410) 226–0191 and rest rooms turn right on Market St.

    Note: The confectionery is an old-time country store that has been run by Myrtle "Mert" Bringman and her son Bill for more than forty years. Mert claims the store is the oldest in Oxford and proudly professes to have made the store's sandwiches every morning for forty-one years. As you may have to wait up to twenty minutes for the ferry located 0.3 mile up the road, you might want to stock up on drinks or have an ice cream cone with Myrtle and Bill.

- 11.8   You'll pass the quaint Towne Shoppe on your right.

- 11.9 Cross Strand St. to reach the Oxford Bellevue Ferry (410) 745–9023 or www.oxfordmd.com/obf.

  Note: The ferry leaves every twenty minutes for a ten-minute ride across Tred Avon River to St. Michaels. Cyclists pay $2 one-way or $3 round trip. (Cars cost $5 and $8). The ferry began in 1683 and is believed to be the nation's oldest privately operated ferry service. The ferry is located next to a private yacht club, providing a nice view of various kinds of boats.

- 11.9 Leave the ferry and ride down the dock to the parking lot. Turn left onto an unmarked road that will curve away from the water. Rest rooms will be on your right as you leave the parking lot.

- 12.3 You'll pass a little country store on your right with drinks and snacks. A makeshift sign advertising antiques immediately follows the store. (This is a lightly traveled road but it lacks a shoulder so be aware of passing traffic.)

- 15.5 Turn left at T intersection onto unmarked road with Royal Oaks general store straight ahead. The country-style Old Creek Sales antique store will be on your left as you make the turn.

- 16.5 Turn left at T intersection onto Rte. 33 West.

- 18.8 You'll pass a sign on the right indicating the town of St. Michaels.

- 19.3 You'll pass a grocery, deli, and flower shop. St. Michaels, which is about two-thirds into the ride, is home to many small shops and bistros and is a nice spot to stop and walk around.

- 19.6 You'll reach Cherry St. and Justina's Ice Cream shop. Look for a sign indicating public rest rooms.

- 19.6 Turn right on Cherry St. to reach the Chesapeake Bay Maritime Museum (410) 745–2916 or www.cbmm.org, St. Michaels Patriot Cruises (410) 745–3100, and the Crab Claw restaurant (410) 745–2900 or (410) 745–9366.

  Note: The Maritime Museum is a large waterfront complex featuring history of the Chesapeake Bay with a collection of traditional water-

craft, a circa 1879 lighthouse, and an area where visitors can crab, tong for oysters, and watch as boatmen restore traditional Bay vessels. Visitors could easily spend an afternoon exploring the museum attractions.

Patriot Cruises is a commercial sightseeing boat that tours area rivers while a guide discusses bay history and wildlife such as ospreys, which make their nests on river channel markers. Tours last one to one and a half hours.

(If you'd like to take a 31.2-mile round trip ride to Tilghman Island, continue west on Rte. 33. In less than 2 miles, you'll reach Rte. 579, which is an 8-mile ride along lightly traveled roads with a water view. Continuing a mile farther on Rte. 33, you'll come to Rte. 451 which will take you on a 2-mile trip to the town of Claiborne and the Rich Neck Manor. The manor was the plantation home of Continental Congress member Michael Tilghman. Following Rte. 33 for 2 more miles, turn left onto a small wharf that harbors one of the last remaining skipjack fleets. Another 2.5 miles brings you to the Coast Guard Station at Black Walnut and the end of this optional section. Turn around and return to St. Michaels along Rte 33E.)

- 20.1 Turn left back onto Scenic Rte. 33 East to head back to Easton.
- 23.1 Cross Oak Creek.
- 27.3 You'll pass an Exxon convenience store on your left.
- 28.4 You'll pass a small wine shop on your left.
- 28.6 Enter Easton
- 29.0 Turn left onto Rte. 322 and ride for 1 block.
- 29.3 Turn right at Marlboro Rd. traffic light and arrive back at Tred Avon Square.

10

Iron Furnace Ramble

Salisbury—Furnace—Colbourne—Salisbury

Bicycling doesn't get much better than it does on this ride, one of the favorites of the Salisbury State University Cycling Club. On this ride—an easy 33-mile meander through woodlands preserved by the Nature Conservancy in Wicomico County in southeast Maryland—the scenery is idyllic, the trees shelter you from prevailing winds, the pavement is smooth, the road is flat, and automobile traffic is light. Ah-h-h!

Just to make life even easier, the cycling club has marked the entire route with white arrows numbered *33* (the length of the ride and the number given it when the club first marked it for the 1989 National Rally of the League of American Wheelmen)—markings that have been kept up to date, notes club representative Joseph K. Gilbert, who contributed and verified this ride. All in all, it's a perfect choice for warming up early in the season or for introducing a novice to the joys of two-wheeled touring.

The nominal destination, Furnace Towne, is a restored iron-smelting village. During summer weekends you might see a blacksmith pounding hot iron on an anvil, a candle-maker dipping wicks into tallow, or a broom-maker assembling straw on a wood handle. Stop long enough in Furnace also to stroll along the 0.25-mile-long nature trail, which leads you into a marsh where discreet signs identify exotic cypress trees and other plants.

Although the starting place of this ride is the university campus, you might prefer instead to begin and end from Snow Hill, a couple of miles southeast of the route on Route 12. There you can make a weekend of it at the Snow Hill Inn (410–632–2102), or the River House Inn (410–632–2722); for further information contact Somerset County Tourism and Visitors Center (800–521–9189 or 410–651–2968) in Princess Anne, Maryland. Outside the town is Pocomoke River State Park (410–632–2566), where those preferring to camp can pitch a tent.

The Basics

Start: Salisbury, at the front of the Maggs Physical Activity Center at Salisbury State University. Parking there is free to the public, although it may be crowded during the school year. To get to the university from Rte. 13, turn west onto Bateman St. and proceed .75 mile.

Length: 33.7 miles.

Terrain: Virtually flat. Mostly on well-paved country roads with very little traffic.

Food: Stock up in Salisbury, because this ride is so rural that there are no places to stop for food or drink unless you make a detour of 4 miles each way to the town of Snow Hill halfway through the ride (adding the detour to Snow Hill lengthens the route to 42 miles).

Miles & Directions

At the start of the ride, follow the big white arrows painted on the pavement until the ride is marked with smaller white arrows numbered 33. When approaching the university on your return route, follow the green arrows marked with an *H* (for *Home*).

- 0.0   Depart from the exit in front of the gym across from the parking lot.
- 0.1   Head straight onto Bateman St. Cross the very busy Rte. 13 (S. Salisbury Blvd.) by using the tunnel underneath it.

- 0.3   Turn right at the T intersection onto S. Division St., which eventually becomes Coulbourne Mill Rd.
- 2.6   Turn right onto Union Church Rd.
- 4.2   Turn right onto Pocomoke Rd., which, after crossing St. Lukes Rd., becomes Stevens Rd.
- 10.4 Turn left onto Old Furnace Rd. (the road is unmarked, but follow the sign pointing to Snow Hill). At mile 16.3 you will pass the Nassawango Iron Furnace on your right; the sign to it faces oncoming traffic. You might like to stop here and wander around the village restoration and the nature trail. There are also public rest rooms and water.
- 17.5 Turn left onto Rte. 12 (Snow Hill Rd.).
  Note: If you wish to visit the town of Snow Hill for lunch or other sightseeing, turn right instead and ride 4 miles; although traffic is moderate, there is a lane-wide paved shoulder.
- 18.1 Turn right onto Mt. Olive Church Rd.
- 24.3 Turn left onto Spearin Rd.
- 27.3 Turn right onto Rte. 12 (Snow Hill Rd.).
- 28.0 Turn left onto Old Fruitland Rd.
- 29.4 Bear right at the yield sign onto the unmarked Coulbourne Mill Rd. After crossing over a bridge, follow the main road as it bears right and joins S. Division St.
- 33.4 Turn left onto Bateman St. Cross Rte. 13 (S. Salisbury Blvd.). Enter the Salisbury State University campus.
- 33.7 Head straight into the Maggs Physical Activities Center parking area.

11

Deal Island Skipjack Challenge

Salisbury—Jason—Deal Island—Princess Anne—
Salisbury

Nautical history buffs particularly ought to enjoy this ride, as its destination—Deal Island in the Tangier Sound—is the home of one of the last remaining skipjack fleets. Skipjacks are sailing vessels that by law may not be motorized. In the nineteenth century they were the primary way fishermen tongued for oysters. Today, at the threshold of the twenty-first century, the dozen or so skipjacks at the small Deal Island harbor are one of the last fleets of the waterman's work boats. If you're lucky enough to time your visit for the proper weekend in the spring, you may be able to cheer on the annual skipjack races; for details call Somerset County Tourism and Visitors Center (800–521–9189 or 410–651–2968) in Princess Anne.

On the way out, in addition to cycling through miles of pastoral farmland of Wicomico and Somerset counties, you'll pedal through the tidal marshland of the Deal Island Wildlife Management Area. Birders might enjoy packing a small pair of binoculars and looking for great blue heron and other shore birds.

On the return the route takes you through the historic town of Princess Anne. There you will ride by the two-century-old

Washington Hotel (410–651–2525), where George Washington's mother once spent the night; if you wish, you can do so today. In the winter the hotel is worth a stop for a steaming bowl of oyster stew; in the spring try the soft-shell crab sandwich. (The weather in this southeastern peninsula of Maryland is so moderated by the surrounding bodies of water that you can comfortably bicycle year-round.)

For the most part the terrain is flat, but don't let that fool you. The land is exposed and there is a significant prevailing wind from the west, and so on the way out "you work," remarks Joseph K. Gilbert, representative of the Salisbury State University Cycling Club, who contributed and verified this ride. But the payoff is that "you have a wonderful tailwind coming home," he adds.

The club designed this ride for the 1989 National Rally of the League of American Wheelmen held at the university, marking the pavement with orange arrows and the number *62* (for its approximate mileage). Where roads have not been repaved since, many of those arrows will still guide you.

Because this route is so rural, services are limited. There are two mom-and-pop stores for buying snacks and drinks in Monie and Deal Island, as well as public rest rooms at the gas station on Deal Island. For those wishing to make the ride into a more leisurely weekend trip, Princess Anne has a number of beautiful bed-and-breakfast inns (again, call Somerset Community Information for suggestions). And Salisbury itself has all the major chain hotels, motels, and restaurants.

The Basics

Start: Salisbury, at the front of the University Center at Salisbury State University. Parking there is free to the public, although it may be crowded during the school year. To get to the University Center from Rte. 13, turn west onto Dogwood Dr. and proceed for 0.2 mile.

Length: 63 miles.

Terrain: Virtually flat, although there can be persistent headwinds on the way out (remember, headwinds have been likened to hills that never quit). Very low traffic, and Rte. 363 has a lane-wide shoulder almost its entire length.

Food: A couple of convenience stores along the way, plus all services in Princess Anne and Salisbury.

Miles & Directions

Note: Follow directions carefully as not every small street is shown on the map. Follow the big orange arrows at the start until the ride is marked with an orange *62* and smaller arrows. When you approach the university on your return, look instead for green arrows marked with an *H* (for *Home*).

- 0.0 Head straight out the exit of the University Center parking lot. Turn left onto Dogwood Dr.; turn right onto Wesley Dr.
- 0.3 Turn right onto unmarked Pine Bluff Rd.
- 0.5 Turn left onto Camden Ave.
- 2.3 Bear right at the Y intersection onto Allen Rd. After you pass through the village of Allen (which has a small convenience store), the road changes its name to Loretto Allen Rd.
- 8.3 Turn right onto Polks Rd. Stop in at Foggy Bottom, a discount store, for delftware and other items; it has "good prices" and "will ship," notes Joe Gilbert.
- 10.3 Turn left onto New Rd.
- 11.5 Turn right at the T intersection onto Ridge Rd.
- 13.7 Turn left at the T intersection onto Mt. Vernon Rd.
- 14.5 Make the first right onto Black Rd.
- 16.6 Turn left at the T intersection onto Drawbridge Rd.
- 17.3 Make the first right onto Fitzgerald Rd.
- 19.8 Turn right at the T intersection onto Rte. 363 (Deal Island Rd.), and stay on it to Wenona Harbor at the very end. At mile

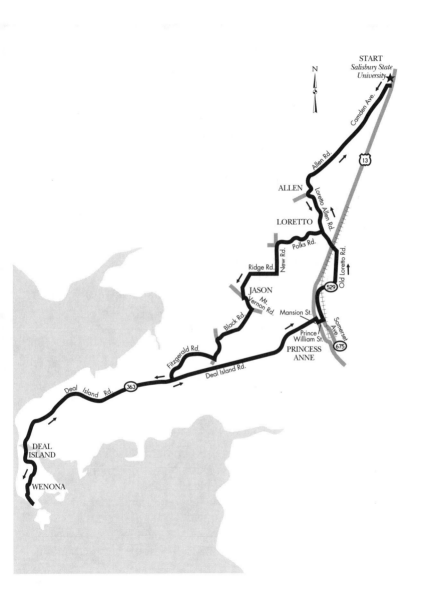

START
Salisbury State
University

N

Camden Ave.

Allen Rd.

US 13

ALLEN

Loretto Allen Rd.

LORETTO

Polks Rd.

New Rd.

Ridge Rd.

Old Loretto Rd.

529

JASON

Mt. Vernon Rd.

Mansion St.

Black Rd.

Prince William St.

PRINCESS ANNE

Somerset Ave.

675

Fitzgerald Rd.

Deal Island Rd.

363

Deal Island Rd.

DEAL ISLAND

WENONA

32.1 you'll reach Deal Island. Stop to explore. To return, turn around and retrace your route, pedaling 18 more miles straight into Princess Anne. At mile 50.3 you'll cross busy Rte. 13.

- 50.4 Turn right onto Mansion St.
- 50.5 Turn left onto Prince William St.
- 50.7 Turn left onto Rte. 675 (Somerset Ave.) and look for the Washington Hotel on your left.
- 52.1 Turn right onto Rte. 529 (Old Loretto Rd.). At mile 54.7 cross Rte. 13. Watch carefully, as the traffic is heavy and there is no traffic light. After this intersection Old Loretto Rd. becomes Loretto Allen Rd.
- 56.9 Bear left onto Allen Rd., which eventually becomes Camden Ave.
- 62.8 Turn right onto Pine Bluff Rd.
- 62.9 Turn left onto Wesley Dr.
- 63.0 Turn left onto Dogwood Dr.
- 63.1 Turn right into the Salisbury State University Center parking lot.

12

Historic Annapolis Ramble

U.S. Naval Academy—Downtown Annapolis—
Susan B. Campbell Park—Quiet Waters Park

Historic and proud, Maryland's capital city has served the state into the new millennium while retaining the character and charm of its 300-year-old roots. This little town by the Chesapeake Bay is known not only for its port city history, but by its stately structures, narrow brick-lined streets, and classic village architecture. It is home to the Maryland General Assembly, the United States Naval Academy, and historic St. John's College founded in 1696.

The ride starts with a pleasant water view across College Creek before passing St. John's College en route to the U.S. Naval Academy. The academy, founded in 1845, is an undergraduate college for 4,000 students who have committed to join the U.S. Navy after graduation. The campus abuts the Severn River and the Chesapeake Bay and provides a colorful view of the water and its many boats. On any given day, midshipmen and women are on the Bay practicing their skills or marching in disciplined formation around the historic campus.

Make sure to visit the Armel-Leftwich Visitors Center (410) 263–6933 before leaving the grounds. The modern visitors center houses an academy museum and provides guided tours of the campus.

After the academy, you'll travel into downtown Annapolis and to the steps of the Maryland State House (410) 974–3400. The 220-year-old State House is the oldest state capitol in continuous use and once served—for about six months in 1783—as the nation's capitol. George Washington resigned as Continental Army commander in the State House, and the Treaty of Paris— ending the Revolutionary War—was ratified there.

Leaving the State House, you'll head to the waterfront and the Susan B. Campbell Park. Because this 19-mile ride can be finished in a couple of hours, you may want to take advantage of the park's charter fishing and touring boats. A visitors center with charter information will be on your left as you enter the park.

After the park, ride up Annapolis' steep but historic red brick Main St. to the circa 1857 St. Anne's Episcopal Church (410) 267–9333 and its prominent steeple, which watches over the city and waterfront. The church, founded in 1,692 and open to the public, houses the Annapolis City clock, which continues to chime every 15 minutes and on special occasions.

The route then winds its way through Annapolis neighborhoods en route to the midway point and 336-acre Quiet Waters Park (410) 222–1777. The park, which is free to cyclists, offers hiking and biking trails, picnic areas with grills, and a scenic overlook of the South River. You can also rent kayaks, canoes, or pedal boats, take a leisurely stroll through the park's formal gardens, or sit down for lunch at the Quiet Waters Cafe. Take your time visiting the sights in the park and along the ride's first half because the return section has few attractions and finishes quickly.

As you ride this route, you may want to read a few directions ahead as the route contains many quick turns within one or two tenths of a mile. Also note that this ride can be very steep and may be rough in spots for out-of-shape riders. Most of the hills, however, are relatively short with plenty of places to stop and rest along the way. This is a popular route for the Baltimore

Bicycle Club, according to member Bill Siwak, who submitted the information on which the ride is based.

For more information about Annapolis' historic attractions call the Historic Annapolis Foundation at (410) 269–0432, or for lodging information call the Annapolis and Anne Arundel County Visitors Center at (410) 280–0445.

The Basics

Start: Annapolis, Maryland State Administrative Offices Building parking lot, Taylor Ave. off Roscoe Rowe Blvd. From Washington, D.C., take Hwy. 50 East to Exit 24 and Roscoe Rowe Blvd. Turn right onto Taylor Ave and right into the parking lot behind the office building. From east of the Chesapeake Bay, take Hwy. 50 west over the Severn River Bridge to the Annapolis exit and Roscoe Rowe Blvd. Turn right onto Taylor Ave. and right again into the office building parking lot. Parking is $4 per day Monday through Friday and free on weekends and holidays.

Length: 19.2 miles.

Terrain: Largely rolling with some tough, steep hills. Many of the tougher climbs are noted in the mileage directions. The route is rideable for most fitness levels, though out-of-shape riders will have occasional difficulty. A large, relaxing park is located midway through the ride and is an excellent spot for tired riders to recover before the return trip.

Food: Snacks, restaurants, and rest rooms are available every couple of miles between miles 4 and 13.5. Individual mileage directions will indicate rest rooms, convenience stores, and restaurants. You may want to stock up toward mile 13.5 as few amenities are available along the ride's last 5.5 miles.

Miles & Directions

- 0.0   Turn left out of the Maryland State Administrative Offices Building parking lot onto unmarked Taylor Ave.

- 0.1   Turn right at the traffic light onto Roscoe Rowe Blvd. The boulevard has a wide shoulder, but use the sidewalk to cross College Creek.
- 0.7   Bear left after the bridge and turn left at the Calvert St. traffic light.
- 0.8   Turn right onto St. Johns St.
- 0.9   Turn left onto College Ave.
- 1.1   Turn left onto King George St. You'll pass historic St. John's College, founded in 1696, and the King Williams School on your left. Cross upcoming bridge on the sidewalk.
- 1.8   Turn right at the traffic light onto Rte. 450E. Traffic is heavy so you may want to ride on the sidewalk. Look for a green sign above the road indicating Gate 8 of the United States Naval Academy.
- 1.8   Turn right into the academy at Gate 8.
- 2.3   Turn left onto McNair Rd. to ride along the Severn River. The 1.5-mile road provides a beautiful view as boats make their way along the river to the Chesapeake Bay, which meets the river at the corner of the academy campus. You'll also see disciplined midshipmen and women as they train in the Bay and march campus roads.
- 3.9   On your left, immediately before the academy exit, will be the Armel-Leftwich Visitor's Center (410) 263–6933. The modern-style center features academy history, campus tours, and a great view of the Chesapeake and its many sailing vessels. The center also has rest rooms and a small restaurant.
- 3.9   Exit the academy through Gate One. Bear left onto East St. (East St. is the second road immediately after the exit and veers at an angle uphill and away from the campus).
- 4.0   Turn right onto King George St.
- 4.0   Turn left onto Maryland Ave. This is a narrow street lined with small antique shops.

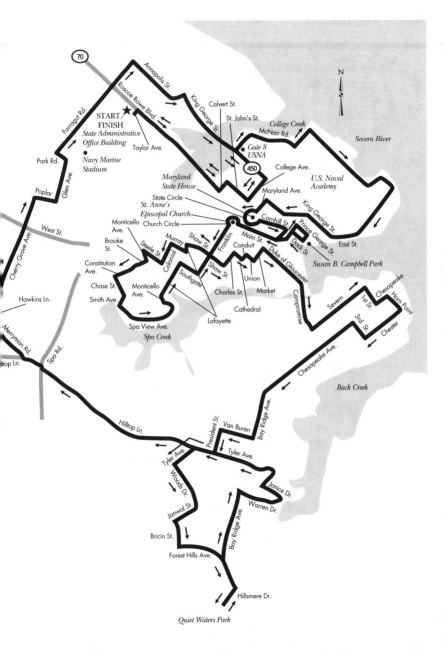

70

START
FINISH
*State Administrative
Office Building*

Roscoe Rowe Blvd

Annapolis St.

Farragut Rd.

Taylor Ave.

Park Rd.

*Navy Marine
Stadium*

Glen Ave.

Poplar

West St.

Cherry Grove Ave.

Hawkins Ln.

Merryman Rd.

Spa Rd.

itop Ln.

King George St.

Calvert St.

St. John's St.

College Creek

McNair Rd.

Gate 8
USNA

450

College Ave.

Severn River

*U.S. Naval
Academy*

Maryland Ave.

*Maryland
State House*

State Circle
*St. Anne's
Episcopal Church*
Church Circle

Cornhill St.

King George St.

East St.

Monticello
Ave.

Murray

Shaw St.

Franklin

Main St.

Prince George St.

Dock St.

Brooke
St.

Steele St.

Colonial

Conduit

Duke of Gloucester

Susan B. Campbell Park

Constitution
Ave.

Southgate

Shaw St.

Union

Chase St.

Monticello
Ave.

Charles St.

Market

Compromise

Chesapeake

1st St.

Horn Point

Smith Ave.

Lafayette

Cathedral

Severn

3rd St.

Chester

Spa View Ave.

Spa Creek

Chesapeake Ave.

Back Creek

Hilltop Ln.

President St.

Van Buren

Bay Ridge Ave.

Tyler Ave.

Tyler Ave.

Woods Dr.

Janice Dr.

Janwal St.

Warren Dr.

Bricin St.

Bay Ridge Ave.

Forest Hills Ave.

Hillsmere Dr.

Quiet Waters Park

N

- 4.1 You'll arrive at State Circle with the Maryland State House (410) 974–3400 directly in front of you. Bear right around the red brick circle.
- 4.2 Turn left at T intersection onto School St.
- 4.3 Turn right onto Cornhill St. and ride down the hill. Bear right at the bottom of the hill to head toward Main St. The Market House Restaurant will be directly in front of you.

  Note: You are now in the heart of historic Annapolis. Feel free to walk your bike along its wide sidewalks and visit its many restaurants and shops.
- 4.5 Turn left onto Main St. Follow the small circle around to the left to the other side of the Market House Restaurant.
- 4.5 Turn right on Dock St. toward Susan B. Campbell Park. A visitors center and rest rooms will be on your left as you enter the park and marina. In addition to a great view, a restaurant, and shady places to rest, the park features numerous eco- and sightseeing charter boats that tour the Chesapeake and nearby Severn and Spa rivers. After visiting the park, follow U-shaped Dock St. across the park, out the other side, and away from the water.
- 4.8 Turn right onto Craig St. behind the visitors center. (Street sign is obscured by a telephone pole on your left).
- 4.8 Turn left onto Prince George St.
- 4.8 Turn left at the traffic light onto Randall St.
- 4.9 Turn right onto Market Space.
- 4.9 Turn left at unmarked T intersection to head back to Main St.
- 5.0 Turn right onto historic Main St. You'll see the steeple of St. Anne's Episcopal Church (410) 267–9333 at the top of the hill at Church Circle. The church, which is open to the public, was founded in 1692 with the present building constructed in 1857. Turn right at the circle and follow the road around to the left.

- 5.4 Turn right—almost all the way around the circle—onto unmarked Franklin St. and continue through the traffic light at Cathedral Ave.
- 5.5 Turn right onto Shaw St.
- 5.6 Turn left onto Lafayette Ave.
- 5.7 Turn right onto Murray Ave.
- 5.8 Turn left at T intersection onto Colonial Ave.
- 5.8 Turn right onto Steele Ave.
- 5.9 Turn left at T intersection onto Monticello Ave. The B & B Mini Mart with drinks and sandwiches will be across the intersection on your left.
- 6.0 Turn right onto Brooke St. and ride up the hill to a small fork in the road. Bear left to cross Amos Garrett Blvd.
- 6.1 Brooke St. will become Constitution Ave. after crossing Amos Garrett Blvd.
- 6.2 Turn left at T intersection onto Chase St. The Maryland Hall for Creative Arts (410) 263–5544 will be directly in front of you.
- 6.3 Turn right onto Smith Ave.
- 6.4 Turn left at T intersection onto Spa View Ave.
- 6.7 Cross Monticello Ave. and follow Spa Circle around to your left.
- 6.8 Turn right onto Monticello Ave.
- 6.8 Take an almost immediate right onto Lafayette Ave. Ride up the hill to a stop sign.
- 7.0 Turn right onto Southgate Ave.
- 7.2 Turn left onto Franklin St. (If you need a rest, pedal straight across Franklin Street to the water about 200 yards ahead.)
- 7.3 After turning on Franklin St., turn right on Shaw St. Follow Shaw St. to the water where it curves left and becomes Charles St. Note the quaint, old houses on your left.
- 7.5 Turn right onto Cathedral St.

- 7.5 Turn left on Conduit St.
- 7.5 Turn right onto Union St.
- 7.6 Turn left at the T intersection onto Market St.
- 7.8 Turn right at T intersection onto Duke of Gloucester St. The Annapolis City Hall will be straight ahead as you make the turn. Farther up you'll pass the Charles Carroll House (410) 269–1737 on your right.
- 8.2 Turn right onto unmarked Compromise St. and ride on the sidewalk across a pleasant, arching drawbridge over Spa Creek. The bridge provides a great view of the water and its many busy docks.
- 8.4 Bear left after the bridge to reach the traffic light at Severn Ave. Turn left onto Severn Ave. The Eastport Clipper restaurant with rest rooms will be on your right. As you ride along Severn Ave. you'll pass numerous restaurants, including the well-known Ruth's Chris Steak House and the more local O'Leary's Seafood Restaurant. The Annapolis City Marina (410) 268–0660 will be on your left. The marina features touring boats, rest rooms, and a restaurant.
- 8.7 Turn right on First St.
- 8.7 Turn left onto Chesapeake Ave.
- 8.8 Turn right near the water onto Horn Point Dr.
- 8.8 Follow the road to the right onto Chester Ave.
- 9.0 Turn right on Third St.
- 9.2 Turn left back onto Chesapeake Ave. (A convenience store will be on your right as you cross Sixth St.)
- 9.8 Chesapeake Ave. will become Bay Ridge Ave. as you bear left at a stop sign beside the Eastport Shopping Center. The center has numerous shops and places to eat and rest.
- 10.1 Turn right onto Van Buren St.
- 10.3 Turn left onto President St. then right at a T intersection onto Tyler Ave. About 300 yards after the T intersection, cross left to continue on Tyler Ave. (This is a fairly busy area so watch for traffic as you make your left turn.)

- 10.7 Turn left on Woods Dr.
- 10.9 Turn right onto Janwall St. and ride up a slight hill.
- 11.0 Turn left onto Bricin St. and continue to the top of a second hill.
- 11.2 Turn left onto Forest Hill Ave.
- 11.4 Turn right onto Bay Ridge Ave. and continue to a large intersection with traffic light and a Crown convenience store on your right.
- 11.6 Cross the intersection as Bay Ridge Ave. becomes Hillsmere Dr.
- 11.7 Turn right onto Quiet Waters Road and continue to 0.3 mile to the entrance of Quiet Waters Park (410) 222–1777.
  Note: You are about halfway through the ride, so this 336-acre park is a great place to rest and spend some time before finishing the route. In addition to water activities, the park offers a summer concert series and an outdoor skating rink November through February. Cyclists enter the park free. (Cars pay $4 dollars.) Stop at the entrance hut for a park map and additional information. Remaining mileage directions exclude touring the park and continue from the park entrance/exit.
- 12.0 Exit Quiet Waters Park.
- 12.3 Turn left back onto Hillsmere Dr. and again cross the large intersection onto Bay Ridge Ave. Bay Ridge Ave. will curve left and uphill with a wide shoulder.
- 13.0 Turn right onto Warren Dr.
- 13.2 Turn left onto Janice Dr. and continue uphill.
- 13.3 Turn right on Tyler Ave. Bear left as Tyler Ave curves around to the traffic light at Bay Ridge Ave. Cross Bay Ridge Ave.
- 13.6 Cross Spa Rd. as Tyler Ave. becomes Hilltop Ln. Look for the Wawa convenience store.
- 15.0 Turn right onto Merryman Rd.
- 15.3 Turn left onto Hawkins Ln.

- 15.4 Turn right onto South Cherry Grove Ave. The avenue will dead-end into a small foot path and wooden bridge. Cross the roughly 25-yard path to continue on South Cherry Grove Ave.
- 15.6 After crossing the path and riding up a small hill, cross West St. to continue on North Cherry Grove Ave.
- 15.7 Turn at right at T intersection onto Poplar Ave.
- 15.9 Turn left at the stop sign onto Glen Ave. (The sign for Glen Ave. is on the far left after the intersection.)
- 16.1 Turn left on Cedar Park Rd.
- 16.4 Turn right on Farragut Rd. You'll pass the Navy–Marine Corps Memorial Stadium on your right.
- 16.6 Cross Roscoe Rowe Blvd. to continue straight on Melvin Ave.

  Note: To cut about 2.4 miles off the ride, turn right on Roscoe Rowe Blvd. back to Taylor Ave and into the State Administrative Building parking lot.
- 17.5 Turn right onto Annapolis St. Follow Annapolis St. to your first traffic light, where you will turn right onto un-marked King George St. at sign reading "Welcome. United States Naval Academy."
- 18.1 Turn right onto College Ave.
- 18.3 Turn right onto St. Johns St.
- 18.4 Turn left onto Calvert St. (The street sign is obscured by a tree.)
- 18.4 Turn right onto Bladen St. Cross back over College Creek on the sidewalk.
- 19.1 Turn left at the traffic light onto Taylor Ave.

13

Maryland Back Country Challenge

Frederick—Buckeystown—Monocacy National Battlefield—Frederick

This short but extremely challenging route through rural and historic Frederick County, MD, is one of the most popular among local cycling clubs. It can be completed in a few hours, but features some thigh-burning climbs as well as mountain views and a bit of Civil War history.

The route begins in quaint downtown Frederick, MD, with its narrow, walkable streets, historic architecture, and small antique shops. Frederick also features the National Museum of Civil War Medicine (301) 695–1864 and the Shifferstadt Architectural Museum (301) 663–3885, which chronicles the life of early German settlers.

After a short trip along the outskirts of town, you'll hit the open country. As you reach the ride's rural section, you'll pedal along a small valley floor entirely surrounded by distant mountains. Small farms, another cyclist or two, and an occasional car are about all you'll see dotting this beautiful landscape. About one-third of the way through the ride make sure to check out Lilypons Aquatic Gardens (301) 874–5133, a large natural aquatic garden supply center and home to annual garden festivals.

A little later, you'll also come to one of Frederick County's main attractions—the Monocacy National Battlefield. This Civil War battlefield was the site of a pivotal fight in which Confederate troops en route to join other Confederate soldiers—with intentions to attack the nation's capital—were stalled just long enough to ruin the Confederate plan.

This Back Country Challenge, however, is known as much for its terrain as its history. The hills around the city of Frederick are extremely steep and rolling. The ride includes fast downhill sections requiring concentration and control, as well as many endurance-testing climbs. The route was included in this book for its test of rider skill and endurance as much as its rolling, mountain views. This loop is a variation on a ride created by the Tourism Council of Frederick County and submitted by its executive director, John Fieseler.

Though this ride is meant to be completed in a single day, you may want to take more time to explore Frederick County's other cultural and historic sites, such as Antietam National Battlefield (301) 432–5124 and the Francis Scott Key Monument/Mt. Olive Cemetery (301) 662–1164.

For lodging or other additional information call the Tourism Council at (301) 663–8687 or (800) 999–3613.

The Basics

Start: Frederick Visitors Center, Church St., Frederick, MD. From Pennsylvania, take U.S. Hwy. 15S to the Rosemont Ave. exit just outside of Frederick. Turn right at the bottom of the exit onto Rosemont Ave. Follow Rosemont Ave. for several blocks before turning right onto Bentz St. Three blocks later turn left onto Church St. The visitors center will be ahead on the left. From Washington, D.C., take Hwy. 270N to Exit 31A/Rte. 85N. Follow Rte. 85N as it becomes Rte. 355N. Rte. 355 will become Market St. in Frederick. Turn right off Market St. onto E. Church St.. The visitors center is just ahead. (Once in Frederick you can also follow the prominently displayed signs directing you to the visitors center.)

Length: 30.5 miles.

Terrain: Very hilly. Though this ride is at least 10 miles shorter than the shortest challenge, its long and difficult climbs qualify the route for the higher difficulty level. Do not be fooled by its short length. This is a challenging ride.

Food: Food, restaurants, and rest rooms are located at the beginning of the ride in downtown Frederick and at miles 0.7, 6.7, 10.6, 18.7, and 29.6. Stock up on water and snacks before the ride as few services are available along this country route.

Miles & Directions

- 0.0   Turn left out of the Frederick Visitors Center parking area onto Church St.
- 0.2   Turn right at the T intersection onto East St.
- 0.4   Turn left onto E. Patrick St.
- 0.7   Pass a 7-Eleven convenience store on your right.
- 0.9   Turn right onto Franklin St.
- 1.1   Turn left at the T intersection onto South St. South St. will become Reichs Ford Rd.
- 3.1   You'll pass Pinecliff Park on your left.
- 3.3   Turn right onto Reels Mill Rd. The scenery becomes very open and picturesque. You will be in a valley here surrounded by mountains. You'll also encounter the first of the ride's challenging climbs.
- 4.8   Use caution as you cross the railroad tracks. Road will veer to your left.
- 4.9   Watch for oncoming cars as you cross this one-lane bridge.
- 5.2   Turn right at the T intersection onto unmarked Ball Rd.
- 6.3   Turn left at the T intersection onto unmarked Rte. 355.
- 6.7   You'll pass the Blue Fox Restaurant on your right.
- 8.0   Turn right immediately before a large stone barn onto Park Mills Rd.

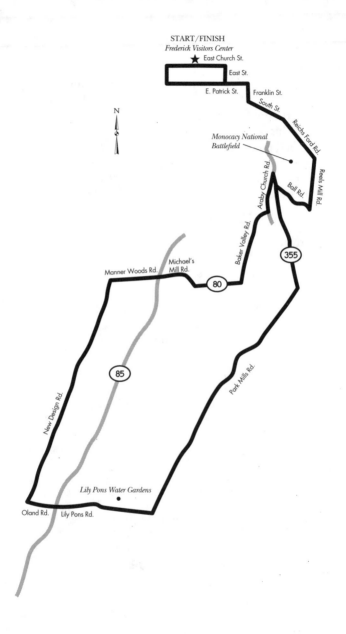

START/FINISH
Frederick Visitors Center
East Church St.

East St.

E. Patrick St.

Franklin St.

South St.

Reichs Ford Rd.

Monocacy National Battlefield

Reels Mill Rd.

Araby Church Rd.

Ball Rd.

Baker Valley Rd.

355

Michael's Mill Rd.

Manner Woods Rd.

80

85

Park Mills Rd.

New Design Rd.

Lily Pons Water Gardens

Oland Rd.   Lily Pons Rd.

N

- 8.5 Cross a highway overpass. Note the open mountain view. Make sure not to go to fast as you ride this steep downhill section.
- 9.1 Cross Rte. 80 at the stop sign to continue on Park Mills Rd.
- 10.6 Flint Hill General Store and Grocery will be on your right.
- 11.0 Careful as you round a sharp curve at the top of the hill. A bright red barn will be ahead on your left.
- 12.4 After crossing a narrow bridge and pedaling up a short climb, turn right onto Lily Pons Rd.
- 13.1 Pass Lilypons Aquatic Gardens and Goldfish (301) 874–5133 on your right.
- 14.0 The ride again opens into a long-range valley view.
- 14.3 Cross Rte. 85 as Lily Pons becomes Oland Rd.
- 15.0 Turn right at the T intersection onto unmarked New Design Rd.
- 16.2 Continue straight through the stop sign at Adamstown Rd.
- 17.1 Use caution as you cross the railroad tracks.
- 17.5 Turn right onto Manner Woods Rd.
- 17.8 Cross another set of railroad tracks.
- 18.7 Cross Rte. 85 as Manner Woods becomes Michaels Mill Rd. in the village of Buckeystown.
  Note: The Buckeystown Market with drinks and snacks is located 100 yards to the left of this intersection. Immediately to your left is the Delight Bakery and Deli. Also at this intersection are Buckeys Antiques and Treasures and Bodmers Pottery.
- 18.8 Buckeystown Pub will be on your left.
- 19.3 Note the Monocacy River to your left.
- 19.6 Careful as the road narrows to one lane.
- 19.7 Buckeystown Park will be on your left. The park offers shade, picnic tables, and grills but no drinking water or rest rooms.

- 20.0 Turn left at the the T intersection onto Rte. 80E.
- 20.1 Cross the Monocacy River.
- 20.9 Turn left onto Baker Valley Rd.
- 22.0 Great elevated view and picturesque farm down and to your left.
- 22.5 The historic Worthington Picnic Area will be on your left.

  Note: The Worthington Picnic Area encompasses the Monocacy National Battlefield, the Worthington House (a restored 1851 farmer's residence from which Confederate Maj. General John C. Breckinridge surveyed his advancing troops during a heated 1864 Civil War battle), and numerous nature trails.
- 23.1 Turn left at the T intersection onto Araby Church Rd.
- 23.2 Pass a Civil War Memorial on your right dedicated to the memory of local regiments.
- 23.6 Turn right at the T intersection onto unmarked Rte. 355. The Monocacy National Battlefield will be directly across the intersection.
- 23.8 Turn left back onto Ball Rd.
- 25.0 Turn left back onto Reels Mill Rd.
- 25.3 Watch for oncoming cars as you cross the one-lane bridge.
- 25.4 Cross the railroad tracks.
- 27.0 Turn left onto unmarked South St.
- 29.1 Turn right onto Franklin St.
- 29.3 Turn left at the T intersection onto E. Patrick St.
- 29.6 Pass the 7-Eleven convenience store on your left.
- 30.3 Turn right onto S. Market St.
- 30.4 Turn right onto E. Church St.
- 30.5 Arrive back at the Frederick Visitors Center (301) 663–8687 or (800) 999–3613.

Virginia

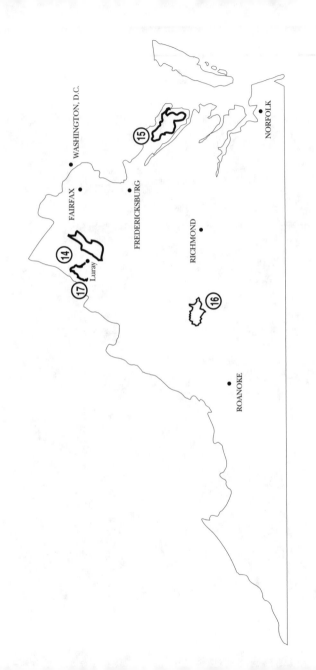

WASHINGTON, D.C.

FAIRFAX

FREDERICKSBURG

NORFOLK

⑮

RICHMOND

⑭

Luray

⑰

⑯

ROANOKE

Virginia

14

Shenandoah Valley–Skyline Drive Classic

*Luray—Thornton Gap—Front Royal—
Browntown—Bentonville—Luray*

This 73.1-mile classic will allow you to explore two of Northern Virginia's most famous areas: the lovely Shenandoah Valley and the northernmost third of the 105-mile-long Skyline Drive, which connects to the 469-mile-long Blue Ridge Parkway. You'll also start the rides less than 1 mile from Luray Caverns (540–743–6551), arguably the most famous caverns in the eastern United States. Another attraction is historic Front Royal, where Stonewall Jackson fought a decisive Civil War battle during his brilliant valley campaign of 1862, and where today the South Fork of the Shenandoah River is considered one of the finest canoeing streams in the East. This route, one of four devised and contributed by Mike Arnette of Powhatan, Virginia, is one of several offered by his commercial outfit, Old Dominion Bicycle Tours (888–296–5036 or 804–598–1808); a group tour with Old Dominion features arrangements made for overnight stays, meals, and mechanical support from a following sag wagon.

The most challenging part of this ride is the 2,000-foot climb up to Skyline Drive, which follows the ridge of the Blue Ridge Mountains. The second most challenging part of the ride is the

30-mile segment preceding the descent into Front Royal, because Skyline Drive gains and loses several thousand feet in altitude as it dances back and forth across both the Appalachian Trail and the border of Rappahannock County and Page and Warren counties. The compensation, of course, is the spectacular vistas alternately to your left and right over the 195,000-acre Shenandoah National Park, which encompasses the full 105 miles of Skyline Drive, along with the lovely dogwoods, redbuds, and rhododendrons that may be in bloom. The speed limit on the Drive is a mere 35 miles per hour—which bikes can exceed on the downhills—and the curvy, forested, two-lane road is well-marked and well-paved. Watch for deer, however, which can bound down out of the hills scarcely 30 feet in front of you! Also, keep your eyes alert for bear.

To take full advantage of the ride's attractions, you might consider breaking the tour into two portions. The first day would consist of a vigorous 42.3-mile challenge with plenty of climbing along Skyline Drive and an overnight in Front Royal (which would also give you a chance to visit Skyline Caverns, 800–296–4545 or 703–635–4545). The second day would be a more relaxing 30-mile cruise back to Luray.

In Luray, possible places to spend the night include the Minslyn Inn (540–743–5105 or 800–296–5105) at mile 1.0, Yogi Bear's Jellystone Campground (540–743–4002 or 800–420–6679) at mile 5.3, and Brookside Restaurant and Cabins (540–743–5698) at mile 6.0; the single campground you'll pass on Skyline Drive— Mathews Arm at mile 20.3—may be closed. In Front Royal try the Pioneer Motel (540–635–4784). Those preferring being pampered at a bed-and-breakfast inn in Front Royal might try the Chester House (540–635–3937 or 800–621–0441), the Killahelin (540–636–7335 or 800–847–6132), or the Woodward House (540–635–7010 or 800–635–7011); seven miles south of Luray, consider Jordan Hollow Inn (888–418–7000 or 540–778–2285) or The Ruby Rose Inn (540–778–4680) in Stanley. For more information, call the local Chamber of Commerce either in Luray

(540–743–3915) or Front Royal (540–635–3185), the Warrenton–Fauquier County Visitors Center (540–347–4414 or 800–820–1021), or the Shenandoah Valley Travel Association (540–740–3132).

The Basics

Start: From Pennsylvania, take I–81 south to I–66 east, to Rte. 240 south. Follow Rte. 340 south into Luray. Turn right onto Rte. 211 (Main St.). The Mimslyn Inn will be 0.5 mile ahead on your left. From Washington, C.D., take I–66 west to Rte. 340 south into Luray. Turn right onto Rte. 211 (Main St.). The Mimslyn Inn will be 0.5 mile ahead on your left.

Length: 72 miles.

Terrain: Ranges from rolling in the Shenandoah Valley to very hilly up to and along the Blue Ridge. There is one 4.7-mile-long climb from Luray (altitude 400 feet) up to Skyline Drive (altitude 2,300 feet); subsequent climbing on Skyline Drive reaches a peak altitude of nearly 3,400 feet. During fall weekends, traffic can be heavy on Rte. 211 from Luray to Skyline Drive; it is generally light along Skyline Drive and in the Shenandoah Valley, excepting for moderate traffic along Rte. 340 back toward Luray.

Food: Many options in Luray and Front Royal. Be forewarned: On Skyline Drive, the only places to get food are the Panorama Restaurant and Store (mile 9.7) just before Thornton Gap and at Elkwallow Wayside (mile 17.4), where there is a grill and camp store; thereafter, it's a 24-mile dry stretch until Front Royal. In the Shenandoah Valley there are scattered convenience stores.

Miles & Directions

- 0.0 Turn right out of the Mimslyn Inn (540) 743–5105 or (800) 296–5105 onto Rte. 211 (Main St.).
- 0.4 Continue straight to remain on Rte. 211 (Main St.).
- 0.5 You'll pass the Luray Visitors Center (540) 743–39l5 on your right.

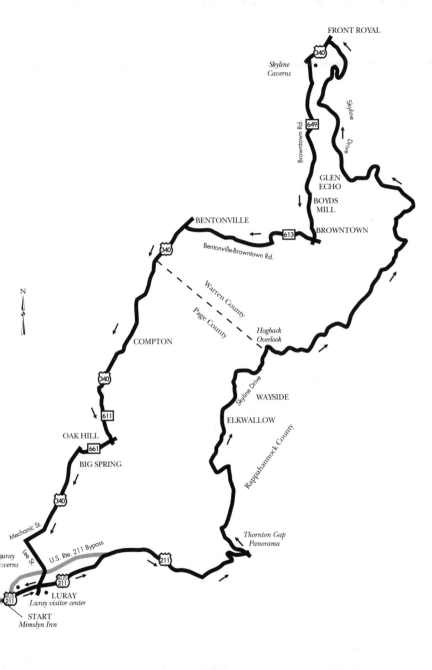

FRONT ROYAL

Skyline
Caverns

340

Brramtown Rd.

649

Skyline
Drive

GLEN
ECHO

BOYDS
MILL

BENTONVILLE

BROWNTOWN

613

Bentonville-Browntown Rd.

340

Warren County

Page County

Hogback
Overlook

COMPTON

N

340

611

Skyline Drive

WAYSIDE

ELKWALLOW

OAK HILL

661

BIG SPRING

Rappahannock County

340

Mechanic St.

uray
verns

Lee St.

U.S. Rte. 211 Bypass

Thornton Gap
Panorama

BUS
211

BUS
211

211

BUS
211

LURAY
Luray visitor center

START
Mimslyn Inn

- 0.6   Use caution as you cross the railroad tracks.
- 1.0   Look for a store where you can stock up on snacks and drinks.
- 1.0+ Continue straight through the traffic light to remain on Rte. 211 (Main St.).
- 1.2   Watch for upcoming grocery and convenience stores.
- 2.1   Use caution and stay to the right as Rte. 211 (Main St.) becomes a divided highway.
- 3.3   Turn right at the T intersection onto Rte. 211 (Lee Hwy.).
- 4.4   You'll pass Yogi Bear's Jellystone Campground (540) 743–4002 or (800) 420–6679 on your right.
- 5.1   Pass the Brookside Restaurant & Cabins (540) 743–5698 on your right.
- 5.3   You may want to grab some bottled water at this store as you are about to begin a 4.7-mile climb.
- 5.8   Rte. 211 becomes three lanes. Stay to the right.
- 6.5   Another of the numerous markets along this section of the ride.
- 9.7   A restaurant and store will be on your right.
- 10.0 Turn left onto Skyline Drive.
- 10.1 You'll reach the Thorton Gap toll area, which cuts through the Shenandoah National Park. At press time, tolls were $5 for bicycles and $10 for automobiles.
- 10.2 Bear left to continue on Skyline Dr. toward the town of Front Royal.
- 13.0 Check out the view from the Beahms Gap Overlook on your left.
- 16.5 Begin your second challenging 4-mile climb.
- 17.4 Pass the Elkwallow Wayside, which has a store and food service. This is your last store until Front Royal.
- 20.6 The Hogback Overlook is a good spot to catch a spectacular view of the Shenandoah River.
- 23.9 Start a third, shorter climb of 1.8 miles.

- 24.4 You'll reach the Range View Overlook.
- 29.3 Start another 1.7-mile climb.
- 33.7 Begin a 1.6-mile climb.
- 34.8 Pass the Gooney Run Overlook on your left.
- 37.0 Pass the Dickey Ridge Visitors Center (540) 635–3566.
- 38.9 Reach the Shenandoah Valley Overlook on your left.
- 41.1 You'll pass the Front Royal toll station (no money necessary).
- 41.7 Turn right at the T intersection onto Rte. 340 (Stonewall
  Jackson Hwy).
- 42.0 Continue straight through the traffic light as Rte. 340 becomes South Royal Ave.
- 42.3 Turn left into the Woodward House Bed & Breakfast
  (540) 635–7010.
  *Note: The Woodward House is roughly half way through the ride
  and is a good place to recover from the day's climbs and get ready
  for the next 31 miles.*
- 42.3 Turn right out of the Woodward House Bed & Breakfast
  (540) 635–7010 onto Rte. 340 (South Royal Ave.).
- 42.4 Continue straight through the next two traffic lights to
  remain on Rte. 340 (South Royal Ave.).
- 43.2 Turn left onto Rte. 649 (Browntown Rd.). You'll pass the
  hamlets of Glen Echo and Boyds Mill, neither of which offers
  services.
- 50.9 Turn right onto Rte. 613 (Bentonville-Browntown Rd.).
- 50.9+ Use caution as you cross this one-lane bridge.
- 56.5 You'll reach the town of Bentonville (no stores).
- 56.6 Turn left at the T intersection onto Rte. 340 (Stonewall
  Jackson Highway). A small store will be 0.1 mile ahead on
  your right.
- 59.4 Enter Page County.
- 61.3 Cross Compton's Run Bridge over a small creek.
- 63.1 Cross Jermiah's Run Bridge.

- 63.2 Turn left onto Rte. 622 (Rileyville Rd.).
- 63.2+ Turn right onto Rte. 611 (Vaughn Summit Rd.).
- 63.3 Cross a small bridge.
- 65.6 Turn right onto Rte. 661 (Sunnyview Dr.).
- 65.6+ Cross again over a small bridge.
- 65.8 Use caution as you cross the railroad tracks.
- 67.2 Turn left at the T intersection onto Rte. 340 (Stonewall Jackson Hwy).
- 69.5 You're almost home, but if you'd like a drink keep an eye out for a small store here.
- 69.6 Cross the Pass Run Bridge.
- 71.2 Cross the Dry River Bridge.
- 72.2 Enter the town of Luray.
- 72.4 Turn right onto Mechanic St.
- 72.8 Turn left onto Lee St. The street sign is often obscured by vines.
- 73.0 Cross Rte. 211 (Main St.) to enter the Mimslyn Inn (540) 743–5105 or (800) 296–5105.
- 73.1 Arrive at the Mimslyn Inn (540) 743–5105 or (800) 296–5105.

15

Northern Neck Multiday Cruise

Montross—Warsaw—Lancaster—Gonyon—
Reedville—Heathsville—Village—Montross

Tucked away in the upper Tidewater, on a peninsula created by the Potomac and Rappahannock Rivers and the Chesapeake Bay, lies Virginia's Northern Neck. Although only an hour from Washington, D.C., it is geographically isolated. Thus, the Northern Neck has been largely bypassed by the inexorable march of twentieth- century progress, with its highways and subdivisions.

What a blessing for cyclists! On this ride through Lancaster, Northumberland, Richmond, and Westmoreland Counties, you'll pedal past homes dating to the late eighteenth and nineteenth centuries, farmhouses in the middle of carefully tended fields, and watermen still using time-honored traditional methods of harvesting fish, crabs, and oysters from the bay and rivers. The byways (not highways) follow old Indian trails and colonial roads, and on the entire peninsula there are only eight traffic lights.

Because of its unique geography, the Northern Neck's history has focused on transportation by sails or steam engines rather than by wheels. Traces of old wharves and turn-of-the-century houses still remain in several riverfront villages. Even today, the

Northern Neck has 12,000 boats registered, so that just about every family has means of putting fresh seafood on the table. Don't miss out on the fresh crabs—especially soft-shell—served at the local restaurants.

The town of Reedville, where you will stay in a restored mansion on the second day of the multiday cruise, is particularly interesting with its Fisherman's Museum (804–435–6529), charter fishing boats, and daily cruises to Tangier Island, where a version of old Elizabethan English is still spoken. For cruise reservations call Tangier Island & Rappahannock River Cruises at (804) 4532–BOAT (2628).

This ride can be enjoyed on your own with the directions and attractions listed below or as a supported tour offered by Virginia tour specialist Mike Arnett of Old Dominion Bicycle Tours (804–598–1808 or 888–296–5036), Powhatan, Virginia. While the route can be ridden as a one-day classic by a strong cyclist, Arnette recommends making at least a long weekend of it to slow down and sniff the roses. As presented, the ride is stretched over three days with a first-day ride of 52.2 miles from Montross to Lancaster, a short 29.3-mile second-day ride from Lancaster to Reedville (leaving time to enjoy Reedville's maritime attractions), and a final-day 51.3-mile ride from Reedville back to Montross. Overnight stays are available at the Inn at Montross (804–493–0573), the Greenwood (804–333–4353) in Warsaw, the Inn at Levelfields (804–435–6887 or 800–238–5578) in Lancaster, and the Bay Motel (804–453–5171) and Morris House Bed & Breakfast (804–453–7016) in Reedville. You can also try camping at Warsaw's Heritage Park Resort (804–333–4038 or 800–335–5564) or Reedville's Chesapeake Bay/Smith Island KOA (804–453–3430).

History buffs, take note: The start at Montross is only a few miles from the birthplaces of both George Washington, in Westmoreland County (804–224–1732), and Robert E. Lee, at the Stratford Hall Plantation (804–493–8038); also in Montross, be sure to check out the historical exhibits at the Westmoreland County Museum and Visitors Center (804–493–8440). The Richmond County Museum (804–333–3607 or 804–394–4901) in Warsaw displays the agricultural history of the region. Lancaster boasts the Mary Ball Washington Museum (804–462–7280), which depicts life over the Northern Neck's 350-year history. In Heathsville, you can watch the restoration of the 110-foot-long Rice's Hotel/Hughlett's Tavern (804–580–3536).

The Basics

Start: Montross, VA, at the Montross Courthouse on Rte. 3. Take I-95 to Fredericksburg and then take Rte. 3E to Montross. The Inn at Montross (804) 493–0573 is directly behind the courthouse.

Length: 69, 105.8, and 132.8 miles.

Terrain: Flat to rolling; traffic is light on most roads, but moderate on Rtes. 3 and 360. Traffic around Reedville can also be heavy on weekends. For the full multiday ride, plan to arrive at Reedville midweek.

Food: Food is available at the Inn at Montross, in the larger towns, and scattered along the ride. Suggestions for when to stock up are made in the "Miles & Directions" section.

Miles & Directions

- 0.0   Turn right out of the Montross Courthouse onto Kings Hwy. (Rte. 3).
- 0.7   Turn left onto Peach Grove Ln. (Rte. 622). Look for a convenience store ahead, where you can stock up on drinks and snacks for the day's ride.
- 1.3   You'll enter Richmond County.
- 2.0   Bear left onto Oak Row Rd. (Rte. 638).
- 4.7   Turn left at T intersection onto Newland Rd. (Rte. 624).

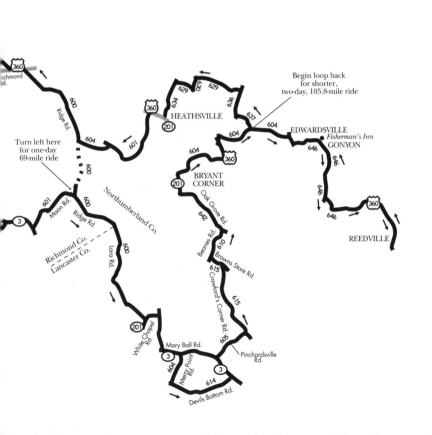

Begin loop back
for shorter,
two-day, 105.8-mile ride

Turn left here
for one-day
69-mile ride

HEATHSVILLE

EDWARDSVILLE
Fisherman's Inn
GONYON

BRYANT
CORNER

REEDVILLE

Northumberland Co.

Richmond Co.
Lancaster Co.

Ridge Rd.

Moon Rd.

Lara Rd.

White Chapel Rd.

Mary Ball Rd.

Merry Point Rd.

Devils Bottom Rd.

Oak Grove Rd.

Beanes Rd.

Browns Store Rd.

Crawford's Corner Rd.

Pinchardsville
Rd.

360

201

3

601

600

604

601

600

600

600

628
629
630
634
636
637
604
604
604
604
642
610
615
615
605
614
646
646
646
646
ichmond
d.

- 5.9 Watch for a second convenience store.
- 12.7 Use caution as you cross a bumpy wooden bridge.
- 13.3 Turn left onto Chestnut Hill Rd. (Rte. 621).
- 15.0 Turn right at T intersection onto Menokin Rd. (Rte. 690).
- 17.9 Turn right onto Main St. (Rte. 3) in the town of Warsaw.
- 18.3 Turn left onto Richmond Rd., which is also Rtes. 360 and 3.
- 19.1 If your supplies are running low, you may want to stock up at this convenience store.
- 19.2 Turn right at the stoplight onto Historyland Hwy. (Rte. 3).
- 24.6 Turn right onto Folly Neck Rd. (Rte. 614).
- 27.1 Turn left to continue on Rte. 614. Folly Neck Rd. will become Beaverdam Rd.
- 27.2 Cross the bridge.
- 29.3 Turn left at T intersection onto Suggetts Point Rd. (Rte. 642) and make an immediate right turn to continue on Suggetts Point Rd.
- 31.2 Turn left at T intersection onto Farnham Creek Rd. (Rte. 608)
- 31.3 Turn right as Farnham Creek Rd. becomes Sharps Rd.
- 32.0 Use caution as you cross another bridge.
- 34.2 Continue straight as Sharps Rd. again becomes Farnham Creek Rd.
- 35.5 Turn right at the stop sign onto Historyland Hwy.
- 37.0 Turn left onto Maon Rd. and look for a small food store.
- 39.9 Bear right at the stop sign onto Ridge Rd. (Rte. 600).
  Note: For a shorter cruise, but a long one-day ride of 69 miles, turn left (instead of right) at this T intersection onto Rte. 600. In roughly 2.5 miles, where Rte. 604 comes in from the right (the first road to your right), keep heading straight on Rte. 600 and pick up the directions from mile 108.9

- 42.1 You'll enter the town of Lara.
- 43.1 Ridge Rd. becomes Lara Rd. as you enter Lancaster County.
- 47.5 Turn left at T intersection onto White Chapel Rd. (Rte. 201).
- 48.0 Bear right onto Courthouse Rd. (Rte. 600).
- 48.2 Bear right again at the yield sign to remain on Courthouse Rd. (Rte. 600).
- 49.7 Turn left at the T intersection onto Mary Ball Rd. (Rte. 3).
- 49.9 Pass the Mary Ball Washington Museum (804) 462–7280.
- 50.1 Keep an eye out for a convenience store.
- 50.3 Pass Lancaster High School.
- 51.9 Turn left into the entrance for The Inn at Levelfields. ·
- 52.2 End the first day's ride with a stay at the Inn at Levelfields (804) 435–6887 or (800) 238–5578.
- 52.5 Turn left out of the inn at T intersection onto Mary Ball Rd. (Rte. 3).
- 53.0 Turn left onto Pinckardsville Rd. (Rte. 605).
- 54.8 Bear left onto Crawfords Corner Rd. (Rte. 615).
- 56.8 Enter the town of Regina.
- 58.3 Turn left to remain on Rte. 615, which becomes Browns Store Rd.
- 59.0 Turn right at T intersection onto Light St. (Rte. 610). You'll pass a convenience store.
- 60.4 Turn left at the stop sign onto Knights Run Rd. (Rte. 642).
- 62.3 Use caution as you cross another wooden bridge.
- 63.2 Continue straight through the stop sign to continue on Rte. 201 near Howland School.
- 63.8 Enter the village of Bryant's Corner.
- 64.1 Turn right onto Indian Valley Rd. (Rte. 604).
- 66.9 Turn left onto Northumberland Hwy. (Rte. 360).

- 67.6 Turn right onto Avalon Ln. (Rte. 604).
- 68.0 Turn right to continue on Rte. 604 as Avalon Ln. becomes Syndors Mill Pond Rd.

  Note: For a shorter total ride of 105.8 miles, and a combined second day ride of 53.6 miles, continue straight on Avalon Ln. (Rte. 604) for 0.1 mile where you will bear right onto Newman's Neck Rd. (Rte. 636). Follow Rte. 636 to Rte. 629, where you will turn left and continue the main ride from mile direction 97.5.

- 71.7 Turn right at T intersection onto Hull Neck Rd. (Rte. 640) in Edwardsville.
- 71.9 Turn left at the cemetery onto Foley Rd. (Rte. 646).
- 73.2 Continue straight on Foley Rd. (Rte. 646) across Rte. 644 at the stop sign.
- 73.4 Remain on Foley Rd. (Rte. 646) as you cross Rte. 645 past a sign indicating the area of Gonyon.
- 75.3 Turn left at T intersection back onto Northumberland Hwy. (Rte. 360).
- 75.4 Turn right onto Brickyard Rd. (Rte. 646).
- 76.3 Turn left to continue on Rte. 646 as Brickyard Rd. becomes Waverly Rd.
- 78.4 Turn right at T intersection onto Northumberland Hwy. (Rte. 360).
- 78.5 Bear left to continue on Northumberland Hwy. (Rte. 360).
- 79.0 You'll pass the Bay Motel (804) 453–5171.
- 80.4 Enter the town of Reedville.
- 80.7 Bear right to continue on Rte. 360, which is now Main St., Reedville. Watch for a convenience store with snacks and drinks.
- 81.1 Pass the Reedville Fisherman's Museum (804) 435–6529.
- 81.5 You'll reach the Morris House Bed & Breakfast (804) 453–7016 and the end of your second day's ride.

  Note: While in Reedville you may want to take a 1.5-hour boat cruise to 3-by-5-mile Tangier Island. The quaint little island is a *step back in time with most of its 800 residents still working the sea. Some still speak a rarely heard form of early modern English. The island is also almost automobile-free and home to some great-tasting soft-shell crab. Tangier Island & Rappahannock River Cruises (804) 453–BOAT (2628) makes one $20 round-trip per day. Charter fishing boats are also available near the Morris House Bed & Breakfast. Ask the inn attendant for directions to the dock.*

- 81.5 Turn left out of the Morris House Bed & Breakfast at the T intersection onto Northumberland Hwy. (Rte. 360).
- 82.3 Bear left to continue on Northumberland Hwy. You may want to stock up on drinks as this is the last convenience store for 20 miles.
- 84.0 You'll enter the town of Lilian.
- 84.6 Turn left onto the Waverly Rd. section of Rte. 646. (Make sure not to turn onto Lilian Ln., which is also a section of Rte. 646.)
- 86.7 Turn right at T intersection where Waverly Rd. will become Brickyard Rd. (Rte. 646).
- 87.6 Turn left at T intersection onto Northumberland Hwy. (Rte. 360).
- 87.7 Turn right as Brickyard Rd. becomes Foley Rd. (Rte. 646).
- 89.6 Continue straight on Foley Rd. through the stop sign in the Gonyon area.
- 91.1 Turn right at T intersection onto Hull Neck Rd. (Rte. 640).
- 91.3 Turn left onto Syndors Mill Pond Rd. (Rte. 604).
- 95.0 Turn right at T intersection onto Avalon Ln. (Rte. 694).
- 95.1 Bear right onto Newman's Neck Rd. (Rte. 636).
- 97.5 Turn left onto Font Hill Rd. (Rte. 629).
  Note: Here is where the shorter 105.8-mile ride rejoins the 132.8-mile main route.
- 99.8 Turn left at T intersection onto Walnut Point Rd. (Rte. 630).
- 100.3 Turn right onto Conewarf Rd. (Rte. 629).

- 101.2 Turn left onto Spring Rd. (Rte. 634).
- 101.9 Use caution as you cross a bridge.
- 103.0 Turn right at the T intersection onto Northumberland Hwy. (Rte. 360) in Heathsville. (To detour to a nearby convenience store, turn left, instead of right, at the T intersection and ride 0.2 mile. Turn around and ride back through the T intersection to continue the ride).
- 103.7 Turn left onto Dodlyt Rd. (Rte. 601).
- 106.2 Bear right at Rte. 604, which will remain Dodlyt Rd.
- 107.4 Bear left at a fork in the road to remain on Dodlyt Rd.
- 108.9 Turn right at T intersection onto Ridge Rd. (Rte. 600).
  Note: Here is where the 69-mile route rejoins the two longer routes.
- 113.6 Turn left onto Richmond Rd. (Rte. 360).
- 114.0 You'll enter the town of Village (No services).
- 114.1 Turn right back onto Ridge Rd. (Rte. 600), which will become Gibeon Rd.
- 116.1 Bear left at the fork to remain on Gibeon Rd. (Rte. 600).
- 116.8 Gibeon Rd. will become Ebenezer Church Rd. as you enter Westmoreland County.
- 120.0 Continue straight across Rte. 203 as Ebenezer Church Rd. becomes Nomini Hall Rd.
- 122.8 Bear right to remain on Nomini Hall Rd. in the town of Kremlin.
- 123.2 Turn left to continue on Nomini Hall Rd., which will become Nomini Grove Rd.
- 125.0 Turn right to continue on Neenah Rd., which is also Rtes. 600 and 621.
- 125.8 Continue straight to remain on Rte. 600 section of Neenah Rd.
- 127.8 Bear left at the fork to remain on Neenah Rd. (Rte. 600).
- 129.2 Turn left onto unmarked Cople Hwy. (Rte. 202).
- 129.2 Turn right onto King's Hwy. (Rte. 3).
- 132.8 Arrive back at the Montross Courthouse.

16

Natural Bridge to McCormick's Farm Challenge

Natural Bridge—Buena Vista—Lexington—Natural Bridge

Southeast Virginia's rolling hills and rural vistas are enough to make any bike ride in the region an enjoyable experience. But throw in a historic military academy, a five-acre vineyard, an historic farm, and one of the seven natural wonders of the world and you've really got something. What you have is the 77.3-mile, two-day, Natural Bridge to McCormick's Farm Challenge.

The challenge begins in Rockbridge County at the site of the 215-foot-high and 150-foot-wide Natural Bridge, considered one of the wonders of the world. The bridge, which forms a stone arch over a flowing creek, is thought to have been created by either an earthquake that caused sections of rock to crumble and fall to the water below, or simply millions of years of water pressure. Either way, the bridge is an interesting quirk of nature worth exploring. You can view the arch through the Natural Bridge Hotel (800) 533–1410, which maintains a walking path and provides nightly symphony and light show performances at the site.

Before beginning the ride, you may also want to visit the 347-foot-deep Natural Bridge Caverns, also on the hotel property, which are among the deepest on the East Coast.

Once on route, the ride's first day will bring you to the quaint village of Buena Vista and past Southern Virginia College. The college served for 128 years as one of the nation's few all-female educational institutions.

At the halfway point, and the optional end of the first day's ride, you'll come to the Osceola Mill Country Inn (540) 377–6455 —an old flour mill converted to an eleven-room bed and breakfast. You may want to stay overnight in order to leave time for the more numerous attractions found along the ride's 40-mile second half.

Day two begins with a trip to Cyprus McCormick Farm (540) 377–2255, the birthplace of one of agriculture's first mechanical inventions. While working these fields in 1831, Cyprus McCormick invented the mechanic grain reaper, which harvested grain five times faster than centuries-old techniques. Today, the farm serves as a research station for the Virginia Polytechnic Institute and State University (Virginia Tech) and features a public museum, gristmill, and restored blacksmith shop.

A few miles later is the Rockbridge Vineyards, (540) 377–6204 or (888) 511–WINE, which offer tours of its five-acre grounds and samples of its awarding-winning wines. (Careful not to drink too much as you still have 36.4 miles to go.)

Toward the ride's end you'll tour the historic town of Lexington, which includes Washington and Lee University (540) 463–8400, as well as the Virginia Military Institute (540) 464–7232. VMI was founded in 1839 and remains the nation's oldest state-supported military college.

A petting zoo is also located along the ride shortly before your return to the Natural Bridge Hotel. The route is divided into two days but conditioned cyclists can complete the ride in one long but grueling afternoon. The difficulty lies in the route's numerous climbs, some of which proved extremely tiring for riders on a recent tour offered by Mike Arnett of Old Dominion Bicycle Tours. Out-of-shape cyclists will want to budget two days for the ride and may have to walk their bikes up the steeper hills, said Arnett, who designed the route.

The region includes other attractions and accommodations not mentioned in this guide.

For more information on the area call the Lexington-Rockbridge Chamber of Commerce at (540) 463–5375.

The Basics

Start: Natural Bridge Hotel, Rte. 11, Natural Bridge, VA, 12 miles south of Lexington, VA, 35 miles north of Roanoke. From the south, take I-81 north to exit 175 and travel 1.5 miles on Rte. 11N. From the North, take I-81 south to exit 180A and travel 2.8 miles on Rte. 11S. From the Blue Ridge Parkway, take the Natural Bridge/Lynchburg exit onto Rte. 130 and follow the signs for 16 miles.

Length: 77.3 miles.

Terrain: This ride is moderately to very hilly and will be difficult for out-of-shape riders.

Food: Restaurants are available at the beginning, middle, and end of the ride. After the first 18 miles, convenience stores are located every few miles along the route. Upcoming stores are noted in the "Miles & Directions" section.

Miles & Directions

- 0.0   Turn right out of the Natural Bridge Hotel (800) 553–1410 or (540) 291–2121, www.naturalbridgeva.com.
- 0.1   Turn right onto Lee Hwy. (Rte. 11).
- 0.2   Turn left at a fork in the road onto Wert Faulkner Hwy. (Rte. 130).
- 0.6   Turn right onto Shafer Ln. (Rte. 608). Watch for loose gravel for the next 2 miles.

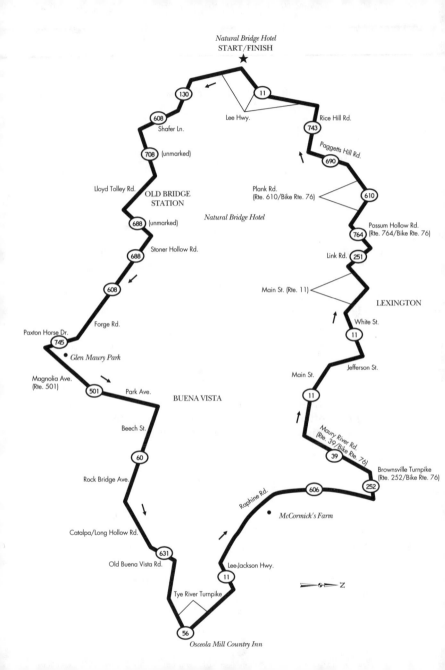

Natural Bridge Hotel
START/FINISH

⑪

⑬⓪

⑥⓪⑧
Shafer Ln.

Lee Hwy.

Rice Hill Rd.
⑦④③

Paggetts Hill Rd.
⑥⑨⓪

⑦⓪⑧ (unmarked)

Plank Rd.
(Rte. 610/Bike Rte. 76)
⑥①⓪

Lloyd Tolley Rd.

**OLD BRIDGE
STATION**

Natural Bridge Hotel

Possum Hollow Rd.
(Rte. 764/Bike Rte. 76)
⑦⑥④

⑥⑧⑧ (unmarked)

Link Rd.
②⑤①

⑥⑧⑧
Stoner Hollow Rd.

Main St. (Rte. 11)

⑥⓪⑧

LEXINGTON

Forge Rd.

Paxton Horse Dr.
⑦④⑤

White St.
⑪

• *Glen Maury Park*

Magnolia Ave.
(Rte. 501)
⑤⓪①
Park Ave.

BUENA VISTA

Main St.

Jefferson St.

⑪

Beech St.

⑥⓪
Maury River Rd.
(Rte. 39/Bike Rte. 76)
③⑨

Brownsville Turnpike
(Rte. 252/Bike Rte. 76)
②⑤②

Rock Bridge Ave.

⑥⓪⑥

Raphine Rd.

• *McCormick's Farm*

Catalpa/Long Hollow Rd.

⑥③①

Old Buena Vista Rd.

Lee-Jackson Hwy.
⑪

Tye River Turnpike

N

⑤⑥

Osceola Mill Country Inn

- 2.2   Be careful of the gravel as you round this sharp curve.
- 2.4   You'll cross a slightly bumpy bridge.
- 2.5   Bear left onto unmarked Gilmore Mills Ln. (Rte. 708), cross the bridge and pass a sign indicating the town of Gilmore Mills.
- 5.1   Turn right onto Lloyd Tolley Rd. (Rte. 773).
- 5.3   You'll pass the once lively rail road town of Old Natural Bridge Station.
- 5.4   Turn left at T intersection onto unmarked Rte. 688. (Do not go under the stone culvert.)
- 5.5   Turn right at T intersection onto unmarked Stoner Hollow Rd. (Rte. 688).
- 7.5   Continue straight through the stop sign to pick up Forge Rd. (Rte. 608).
- 8.0   Continue straight through another stop sign to remain on Forge Rd. (Rte. 608).
- 16.4 Turn right onto Paxton Horse Dr. (Rte. 745).
- 16.8 Paxton Horse Dr. will become West 10th St. as you enter the town of Buena Vista.
- 17.7 You'll pass Glen Maury Park and cross the Maury River.
- 17.9 Watch for trains as you cross the railroad tracks.
- 18.0 Turn left onto Magnolia Ave. (Rte. 501).
- 18.2 Now might be a good time to stop for lunch as you'll pass a few local restaurants.
- 18.8 If you missed the restaurants, pick up a snack at this convenience store.
- 19.3 Bear left to continue on Rte. 501 as Magnolia Ave. becomes Park Ave.
- 19.5 You'll pass Southern Virginia College (540) 261–8400.
- 19.5+ Bear right at the yield sign to continue on Rte. 501 and merge with Beech St. (Rte. 60). Watch for heavy traffic.
- l9.6 Ride straight through the traffic light to continue on Rockbridge Ave. Look for the Kling School sign.

- 20.1 Turn left at the stop sign and Kling School sign onto Catalpa Ave.
- 20.5 Continue straight as Catalpa Ave. becomes Long Hollow Rd. (Rte. 631).
- 20.7 A convenience store will be just ahead.
- 21.8 Bear left onto Old Buena Vista Rd. (Rte. 631).
- 23.0 Cross railroad tracks.
- 23.3 Turn right onto South River Rd. (Rte. 608) and enter the town of Mountain View. Watch for a convenience store.
- 24.5 Enter the town of Riverside.
- 25.2 Note the flowing Twin Falls waterfall on your left.
- 26.1 Another of the ride's many spots to stop for refreshments.
- 26.2 Enter the town of Cornwall.
- 29.3 Enter the town of Midvale.
- 31.7 Enter the town of Marlbrook.
- 34.6 Use caution as you cross the railroad tracks.
- 36.5 Turn left at T intersection onto Tye River Tnpk. (Rte. 56) in the town of Vesuvius.
- 37.2 Arrive at the Osceola Mill Country Inn (540) 377–6455 and the end of the first day's ride.
- 37.2 Turn right out of the inn back onto Tye River Tnpk. (Rte. 56). You will immediately encounter a tough 0.9-mile climb—the most difficult climb of the day.
- 37.6 You'll pass beautiful Glen Falls on your left. This is about halfway up the climb and a good spot to rest.
- 37.9 Enter Augusta County.
- 38.1 Turn left onto Lee-Jackson Hwy. (Rte. 11).
- 38.2 Turn right onto Raphine Rd. (Rte. 606).
- 38.7 Turn right onto McCormick's Farm Dr. (Rte. 918).
- 38.9 You'll pass McCormick's Farm (540) 377–2255.
- 39.1 Enter Rockbridge County.
- 39.3 Turn right onto Raphine Rd. (Rte. 606).

- 39.7 You'll pass some good spots to grab a soda or water.
- 39.8 Use much caution as you approach the heavily trafficked I–81 interchange.
- 40.1 You'll enter the town of Raphine.
- 40.4 Another convenience store is located here.
- 40.9 Pass Rockbridge Vineyards (540) 377–6204 or (888) 511–WINE.
- 43.1 The road gets a little bumpy in this area.
- 43.7 Turn right onto Wade's Mill Loop.
- 43.9 You'll pass Wade's Mill & Buffalo Creek Herb Farm (540) 348–1400.
- 44.0 Turn right onto Raphine Rd. (Rte. 606).
- 44.8 Turn left at T intersection onto Brownsville Tnpk. (Rte. 252/Bike Rte. 76).
- 46.2 Enter the town of Brownsburg.
- 50.4 Enter the town of Bustleburg.
- 51.7 Bear left at the fork in the road onto Maury River Rd. (Rte. 39/Bike 76).
- 52.9 You'll pass the first of numerous stores scattered over the next 10 miles.
- 58.1 You'll pass the Virginia Horse Center (540) 463–2194. The center hosts horse shows and other equestrian activities. Call for times and dates.
- 59.0 Turn right onto Lee Hwy. (Rte. 11).
- 59.5 Pass another convenience store.
- 60.1 Cross the Maury River into Lexington as Lee Hwy. becomes Main St. Drinks and snacks are available in town.

   Note: Lexington is one of the ride's main attractions with the Virginia Military Institute and George Marshall Museum (540) 463–7103. Lexington is also home to Washington and Lee University, as well as various bed and breakfasts, shops, and restaurants. For more information call the Lexington-Rockbridge Chamber of Commerce at (540) 463–5375.

- 60.2 Bear right to continue on Main St. (Rte. 11).
- 60.7 You'll pass historic Virginia Military Institute (540) 464–7232.
- 61.0 Bear right onto Jefferson St. (still Rte. 11).
- 61.1 Pass Washington and Lee University (540) 463–8400.
- 61.5 Turn left at T intersection onto White St. (also Rte. 11)
- 61.6 Turn right onto Main St. (Rte. 11).
- 62.0 Bear left to continue on Main St. (Rte. 11/Bike Rte. 76).
- 62.3 This is the last convenience store for the final 15 miles.
- 62.4 Turn right at the traffic light onto Link Rd. (Rte. 251/Bike Rte. 76).
- 62.7 Link Rd. will become Thornhill Rd. (remains Rte. 251).
- 64.1 Turn left onto Possum Hollow Rd. (Bike Rte. 76).
- 65.2 Bear right at a fork in the road onto Plank Rd. (Rte. 610/Bike Rte. 76).
- 66.0 Bear left where the road forks to remain on Plank Rd. (Rte. 610/Bike Rte. 76).
- 67.2 Cross the bridge.
- 70.7 Cross a slightly bumpier wooden bridge.
- 72.2 Turn left onto Paggetts Hill Rd. (Rte. 690).
- 74.7 Turn right at the T intersection onto Herring Hall Rd. (Rte. 686).
- 75.3 Bear left at a fork in the road onto Rice's Hill Rd.
- 76.1 Turn right at T intersection onto Lee Hwy. (Rte. 11).
- 77.0 You'll reach the Natural Caverns entrance (800) 553–1410 or (540) 291–2121, www.naturalbridgeva.com.
- 77.3 Arrive back at the Natural Bridge Hotel (800) 553–1410 or (540) 291–2121, www.naturalbridgeva.com.

17

New Market to Luray Cruise

New Market—Mt. Jackson—Edinburg—Luray

Historic, natural, and challenging are the best words to describe this medium-distance cruise through the West Virginia countryside. This pleasant, 38.6-mile ride takes cyclists past some of the state's most noted Civil War battlefields, up some of the Mid-Atlantic's toughest hills and, with a little detour, into the East Coast's largest natural caverns.

The trip begins in the historic town of New Market, famous as the site of the last Confederate victory of the Civil War. The three-hour battle was fought on May 15, 1864 and included soldiers from near by Virginia Military Institute. Those soldiers and other elements of the battle are immortalized at New Market's Battlefield Historic Park and Hall of Valor Museum (540) 740–3102, the Museum of the American Cavalry (540) 740–3959, and the Battlefield Military Museum (540) 740–8065. Cyclists interested in additional history and period crafts may want to plan their rides during the annual Heritage Days Festival, Oct. 23 and 24, when New Market's main street fills with old time crafters, or Mother's Day weekend, when VMI students reenact the battle. Call the museums or the New Market Chamber of Commerce (540) 740–3212 for more information.

New Market is also home to the unique Bedrooms of the U.S. Museum (540) 740–5312 which showcases eleven historically accurate period bedrooms from 1630 to the Art Deco style of the 1930s. Even older, and possibly more ancient than the hills you'll ride over, are the area's natural caverns, which draw tens of thousands of visitors per year. New Market is home to the unique rock formations of the Endless Caverns (540) 740–3939 and you can find the Shenandoah Caverns (540) 477–3115 or (888) 4–CAVERNS about 7.5 miles into the ride.

At ride's end, you can explore the Luray Caverns, with soaring ten-story ceilings, towering stone columns, and crystal-clear pools. Bicycle tour operator Mike Arnett, who contributed this ride and who visits the caverns regularly, says the Luray Caverns among the most interesting he has seen. The Luray Caverns were discovered and have been operating as a tourist attraction since 1878. All three caverns sites are open year-round, but hours vary. Call the caverns for more information.

After riding all day and exploring the Luray Caverns, the extremely challenging 36-mile return trip may be too much for many cyclists to complete in one day. The return ride includes a 3-mile climb Arnett considers one of the toughest in the Mid-Atlantic region. It is not a trip for the out-of-shape cyclist. Even well-conditioned cyclists are often forced to dismount and walk up the incline, Arnett said. To provide a rest, the ride ends at the Mimslyn Inn (540) 743–5105 or (800) 296–5105, known as the Grand Old Inn of Virginia.

For those who would like to spend a couple of days cycling the area and visiting local attractions, prearranged tours with accommodations, bicycle guide, and mechanical support can be arranged through Arnett's Old Dominion Bicycle Tours (540) 598–1808 or (888) 296–5036. Riders who prefer to make their own arrangements can choose from numerous accommodations in New Market, including The Quality Inn (540) 740–3141 where the ride begins, the Budget Inn (800) 296–835), the Days Inn (540) 740–4100, and the Best Western (540) 477–2911.

Campsites in New Market are available at the Endless Caverns Campgrounds (540) 740–3993 or nearby Rancho Campground (540) 740–8313.

The bicycle-friendly Cross Roads Inn (540) 740–4157 or (888) 740–4157 and Red Shutter Farmhouse (540) 740–4281 bed and breakfasts provide a third, more cozy alternative in New Market. More information can be had from the New Market Chamber of Commerce (540) 740–3212.

Besides the Mimslyn, accommodations in Luray include Yogi Berra's Jellystone Campground (540) 743–4002 or (800) 420–6679 and Brookside Restaurant and Cabins (540) 743–5698. Call the Luray Chamber of Commerce (540) 743–3915 or Shenandoah Valley Travel Association (540) 740–3132 for more information.

The Basics

Start: The Quality Inn on Rte. 211 in New Market. Coming from Washington, D.C. take Interstate 81 south to Exit 264. Turn left onto Rte. 211 into New Market. From Richmond, VA, take Interstate 64 to I–81 north to exit 264. Turn right onto Rte. 211 toward New Market. The Quality Inn sign can be seen clearly from Rte. 211.

Length: 36 miles each way with sleeping accommodations at both ends.

Terrain: The trip from New Market to Luray provides a couple of moderate climbs. The return trip, however, includes a 3-mile climb that many conditioned riders are unable to complete without walking. The return ride is not for out-of-shape cyclists.

Food: Food and refreshments are available in New Market with additional restaurants and stores periodically along the route. Refreshments can be had at miles 5.5, 20.4, and 20.7, with a restaurant along the ride in Edinburg. An antique dining room awaits riders at the Mimslyn Inn.

Miles & Directions

- 0.0   Leave Quality Inn.
- 0. l   At stop sign, turn right onto Old Cross Rd. (Rte. 211).
- 1.1   Turn right onto Plains Mill Rd. (Rte. 953).
- 1.5   Turn right onto River Rd. which is also Rtes. 728 and 617.

- 1.6 Ride straight on River Rd.
- 3.1 Use caution as you cross the railroad tracks.
- 4.8 Continue straight on River Rd., which becomes Rte. 616 at the yield sign.
- 5.2 Road name changes to Ridge Rd. as you enter the town of Quicksburg.
- 5.5 Turn left to stay on Ridge Rd.
- 5.5+ Turn left on Quicksburg Rd. A little past the 5.5 mile mark you'll see a general store with drinks and snacks.
- 6.3 Turn right onto Turkey Knob Rd. (Rte. 698).
- 7.6 At this point you will reach an optional turnoff for the Shenandoah Caverns (540) 477-3115, one of a number of underground attractions in the area and a prelude to the nationally recognized Luray Caverns at ride's end. The 2-mile road to the Shenandoah Caverns is unmarked Rte. 730 East. You will turn right onto Rte. 730 immmediately before an apple orchard. On the return trip, the caverns will be marked with a sign on your left where you will turn left onto the same road.
- 10.1 Head straight as Turkey Knob Rd. (Rte. 698) changes to Oxford Drive. You will enter the small town of Mt. Jackson, where antique hunters may want to spend some time scouring the local shops.
- 10.3 Immediately into Mt. Jackson, you will cross a wooden bridge over a small creek.
- 10.4 Turn right at T intersection onto Bryce Blvd. (Rte. 263).
- 10.6 Turn left onto Rte. 11, which is Main St. of Mt. Jackson.
- 10.8 Turn right onto Daniel Gray Drive (Rte. 698).
- 14.9 Continue straight as Rte. 698 changes to Palmyra Church Rd.
- 15.6 Bear left to remain on the unmarked Palmyra Church Rd.
- 19.1 You'll arrive at the town of Edinburg and the ride's halfway point. Edinburg is a good place to stop for a rest and lunch with a restaurant about a mile into the town.

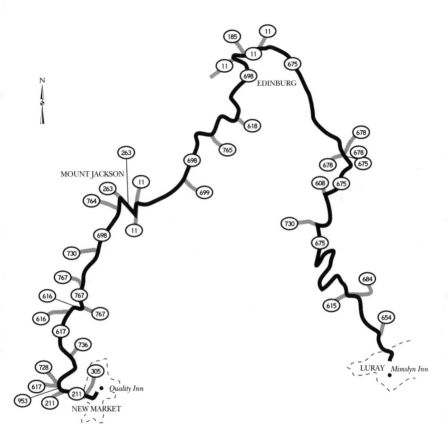

N

11
185
11
675
11
698
EDINBURG
618
678
765
678
678
675
698
263
608
675
MOUNT JACKSON
263
11
699
764
730
698
675
11
730
767
684
616
767
615
654
616
767
617
736
728
LURAY Mimslyn Inn
305
617
211
953   211   Quality Inn
NEW MARKET

- 19.9 Turn right at T intersection onto Old Valley Pike (Rte. 11).
- 20.4 Rte. 11 changes to Edinburg's Main Street and here you will find a good lunch restaurant and store. You may want to order your food to go and sit under a tree in the upcoming George Washington and Jefferson National Forests (888) 265–0019 or (540) 265–5100.
- 21.1 Turn right onto Edinburg Gap Rd. (Rte. 675).
- 23.4 Enter George Washington and Jefferson National Forests and what promises to be a challenging 2-mile climb.
- 25.4 If you're not too busy enjoying the relaxation of coasting downhill, keep your eyes open for a natural spring on the left side of the road. Cyclists often stop to refill their water jugs.
- 26.7 Turn right onto Fort Valley Rd., also known as Rtes. 675 and 678.
- 26.8 Bear left to remain on Fort Valley Rd.
- 27.3 Bear left again at fork in the road to remain on Rte. 675, which becomes Camp Roosevelt Rd.
- 30.1 Once again bear to your left on Camp Roosevelt Rd.
- 30.3 You will pass Camp Roosevelt Recreation Area, which provides primitive camping sites and is a nice place to rest.
- 30.4 Remaining on Roosevelt Rd., you will enter Page County and begin the ride's second mile-long climb.
- 34.6 Turn left to remain on Rte. 675 which will now be called Egypt Bend Rd. Watch for loose gravel. It is here on the return trip that you will begin your extremely challenging 3-mile climb.
- 35.1 Turn right to remain on Rte. 675 which is known locally as Bixlers Ferry Rd.
- 37.8 You'll now enter the town of Luray.
- 38.3 Turn right on Lee St.
- 38.5 Cross Main St. and back to the Mimslyn Inn.

Washington, D.C.

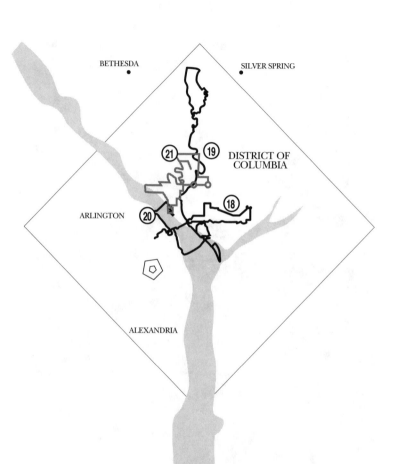

BETHESDA

SILVER SPRING

DISTRICT OF
COLUMBIA

ARLINGTON

ALEXANDRIA

㉑ ㉚ ㉙ ㉘

Washington, D.C.

18

Washington Monuments Ramble

Washington, D.C.—Arlington, VA—Washington, D.C.

The Washington Monuments Ramble is an easy and leisurely way to take in some of the Capitol City's best vistas and most historic sights. This flat, 20-mile ride can be completed in a matter of hours or in days with time spent exploring its many attractions, including the Lincoln and Jefferson Memorials, the Smithsonian Institute, the U.S. Capitol Building, the Supreme Court, and the National Gallery of Art.

The route meanders along the breezy Potomac River, under the shade trees of the Tidal Basin, past the waterfalls of the new Franklin Delano Roosevelt Memorial, and to the base of the towering Washington Monument. You'll also ride to the entrance of the Arlington National Cemetery, where an afternoon can be spent walking your bike among the immaculately kept grounds or contemplating the Tomb of the Unknown Soldier.

The ramble begins at the Thompson Boat Center (202) 333–4861, where bicycles are rented by the day and hour March through November. Before leaving the boat center, check out the adjacent Georgetown Waterfront. Warm weekends fill the waterfront with outdoor restaurants, families, boats parked along the brick walkway, and people watchers taking in the atmosphere. The Monuments Ramble loops back and ends at the boat center, so the Waterfront is an ideal place to end a day of riding with a cold drink, departing boats, and the setting sun.

But, before the rest comes the ride.

The route leaves the boat center and travels along the Potomac River with views of distant bridges, and the Kennedy Center (800) 444–1324 and infamous Watergate Hotel to your right. You'll then ride through the new FDR Memorial and East Potomac Park along the Washington Channel. The park provides views of the channel's many boats and the Potomac River before you loop back toward the Tidal Basin and Jefferson Memorial (202) 426–6822. The roughly circular Tidal Basin is home to thousands of cherry trees and dogwoods, which bloom in early April and are celebrated with a week-long Cherry Blossom Festival (202) 619–7222.

You'll then cross a long bridge into Virginia where you can explore, on foot, the Arlington National Cemetery (703) 607–8052 or take a short loop to view the bronze Iwo Jima Marine Corps Memorial (703) 289–2530 and a bell tower donated by the government of the Netherlands. Observers are allowed to climb the three-story Carillon tower to meet the guest bell musicians who perform regularly May through August. Show times are listed at the tower.

The ride continues over the majestic Arlington Memorial Bridge to the Lincoln Memorial (202) 426–6895 and along the National Reflecting Pool. The view from the top of the Lincoln Memorial is among the most photographed in the city, with the reflecting pool leading to the Washington Monument and the Capitol Building dome in the distance. Riders will follow that view along the pool to the Washington Monument before reaching the grounds of the U.S. Capitol Building. Visitors can tour the Capitol Building's soaring rotunda or watch the House of Representatives or Senate conduct the nation's business.

After the capitol, the ramble takes riders to the fully-restored Union Station train depot (202) 371–9441. The depot is home to grand, old-world architecture as well as numerous shops and restaurants. It's a good place to stop for lunch or a rest before beginning the last few miles of the ride. A few turns later and you'll pass the final attraction of the day—the White House (202) 456–2200—before heading back to the Potomac River and the Thompson Boat Center.

This route is loosely based on two routes found in Michael Leccese's best-seller, *Short Bike Rides in and around Washington, D.C.* (The Globe Pequot Press, third edition, 1996). The new ride, however, includes numerous shorter options and directions for reaching the Iwo Jima Marine Corps, Vietnam, and Franklin Delano Roosevelt Memorials.

The ride is almost entirely flat, with only a few sections of traffic and is suitable for beginning or out-of-shape riders.

The Basics

Start: Washington, D.C., at the Harry T. Thompson Boat Center near the intersection of Virginia Ave. and Rock Creek Potomac Parkway, NW. From Maryland or northern sections of the city, take the parkway directly to the center parking lot. From the National Mall, follow Virginia Ave. to reach the center parking lot. Bicycles are rented from the boat-center building, which is near the water behind and to the left of the parking lot.

Length: A little over 20 miles and can be combined, as noted below, with the Rock Creek Park Cruise for a total of 36.8 miles.

Terrain: For the most part flat, except for short climbs to the Washington Monument and Capitol Building. Traffic is largely avoided along paths or sidewalks, but portions of the ride can include heavy traffic.

Food: Food and rest rooms are available at the boat center and Georgetown Waterfront and many spots along the ride, including the memorials, the Mall, and Union Station.

Miles & Directions

- 0.0   Turn right (southeast) out of the Harry T. Thompson Boat center onto the bike path heading toward the Watergate. The Potomac River will be on your right with the Kennedy Center for the Performing Arts and the Watergate on your left.
- .67   Turn left across the road and away from the water to continue on the bike path beside volleyball courts and a park.
- 1.16 Note the Ericsson Statue on your left. The ride eventually loops back to this point before returning along path to the boat center.
- 1.40 Watch for a sign indicating the FDR Memorial to your left.
- 1.45 About 25 yards past the sign, turn left across Ohio Dr. going away from the water toward the memorial on West Basin Drive.

  Note: If you would rather skip the FDR Memorial, continue straight on the path for about 0.4 mile until you cross a small bridge facing a circular flower garden. Skip to mileage direction 2.03 to continue to East Potomac Park and the Washington Channel.

- 1.52 Turn right passed small, stone pillars onto the 7.5 acre memorial grounds. Rest rooms and a gift shop will be on your left as you reach the memorial entrance. Dismount and walk your bike the rest of the way through. The memorial is divided into four outdoor galleries, one for each of FDR's terms in office. His words are etched in the memorial's walls along side statues representing the condition of the country during each of his terms. The memorial also features many small waterfalls and pools that cool passersby and block out noise from the city.
- 1.80 Get back on your bicycle and follow the light-colored path away from the memorial back to Ohio Dr.

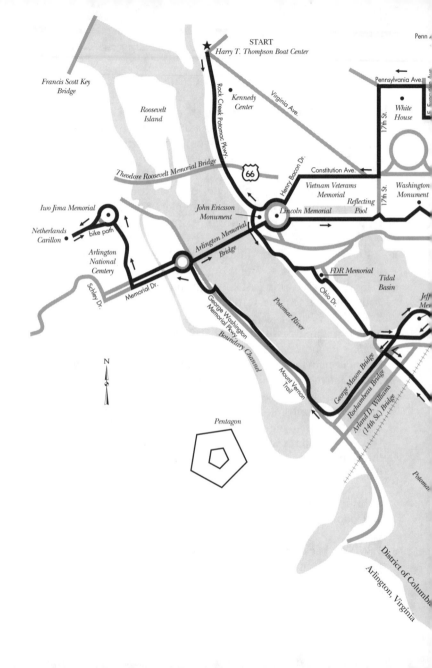

START
Harry T. Thompson Boat Center

Penn

Francis Scott Key Bridge

Roosevelt Island

Pennsylvania Ave.

Kennedy Center

Virginia Ave.

17th St.

White House

Rock Creek Potomac Pkwy.

Theodore Roosevelt Memorial Bridge

66

Henry Bacon Dr.

Constitution Ave.

Vietnam Veterans Memorial

17th St.

Washington Monument

Iwo Jima Memorial

John Ericsson Monument

Lincoln Memorial

Reflecting Pool

Netherlands Carillon

bike path

Arlington Memorial

Arlington National Cemetery

Bridge

FDR Memorial

Tidal Basin

Schley Dr.

Memorial Dr.

Ohio Dr.

Jeff Mer

George Washington Memorial Pkwy.

Potomac River

Boundary Channel

George Mason Bridge

Mount Vernon Trail

Rochambeau Bridge

Arland D. Williams (14th St.) Bridge

N

Pentagon

Potomac

District of Columbia

Arlington, Virginia

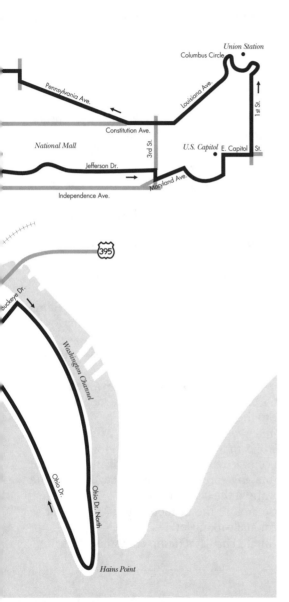

- 1.97 Turn left onto Ohio Dr. immediately crossing a small bridge.

- 2.03 After the bridge, turn right at the circular flower garden. The garden is remnant of a city beautification effort begun by First Lady Helen Taft in 1905.

  Note: If you would rather skip the 4.2-mile ride along the Washington Channel in favor of the Jefferson Memorial, turn left here and follow the bike path along the Tidal Basin to the memorial. Skip to mileage direction 6.27 to continue toward the Jefferson Memorial.

- 2.48 Turn left at the stop sign onto Buckley Dr.

- 2.83 Turn right on Ohio Drive North to follow the loop around East Potomac Park and Hains Point. The park offers a beautiful view of Washington Channel boats and an open vista from the tip of Hains Point. Bikes are permitted on the path at water's edge; however, riding is difficult because of the numerous fishing poles leaning across the path. Walking your bike along the water should allow a nice view and avoid accidents.

- 4.37 You'll arrive at the tip of the loop, known as Hains Point, and the famous 1980 Stewart Johnson statue, *The Awakening.*

- 4.37 Passing *The Awakening*, you will head back along the Potomac River.

- 5.54 A circular rest room building with a water fountain will be on your right. Continue straight out of the loop and back along Ohio Drive to the circular flower garden.

- 6.27 Cross an unmarked road at the flower garden to continue along the bike path lining the Tidal Basin toward the Jefferson Memorial. Proceed around the front of the memorial near the water, making sure to note the foliage lining the basin and the view from the memorial steps.

- 6.63 As you circle around the memorial, turn left to exit as you reach the memorial parking lot.

- 6.67 Turn right toward circular refreshment stand.

- 6.71 Turn left across the road at the memorial parking lot entrance near refreshment stand. You will continue on a bike path uphill and to your right leading to the 14th Street Bridge. The bridge is also known as the George Mason Memorial Bridge.
- 7.32 Leave the bridge bearing right along the bicycle path. Turn left at path T intersection.
- 7.47 Ride up an incline to a small bridge with a nice open view of the Tidal Basin and Jefferson Memorial.
- 7.52 Bear right immediately after the bridge along the path toward the water.
- 8.31 Bear left at a fork in the path shortly before the Arlington Memorial Bridge to cross the highway toward the Arlington National Cemetery.
- 8.46 Cross highway again and make a left about 100 yards later. A section of the Arlington Memorial Bridge will be to your right with a traffic circle and second bridge section to your left.
- 8.47 Cross the highway toward the second bridge.
- 8.64 Cross the bridge on the left sidewalk.
- 8.94 This is as far as you can go on bicycles as the cemetery no longer allows cycling on its grounds. You can dismount, however, and walk your bike through the cemetery to view John F. Kennedy's grave site and the Tomb of the Unknown Soldier.

  Note: If you would like to continue riding, you can take a 1.7-mile loop to view the Iwo Jima Marine Corps Memorial and three-story Carillon Bell Tower given to the United States by the Netherlands to commemorate the two countries' allegiance during World War II. To skip the Iwo Jima loop, turn your bike around and head back toward the Arlington Memorial Bridge. Jump to mileage direction 10.95 to continue to the Lincoln Memorial.

- 8.94 To view the Iwo Jima Memorial, turn right across the road. About 25 yards back toward the bridge will be a road marked "Exit." The road will have a bicycle path on the left side. Turn left onto that path and follow around and up a small hill to an intersection.

- 9.34 Turn right off the path and continue along the road leading to the Iwo Jima Marine Corps Memorial.

- 9.64 Circle around to the back of the memorial and look for the opening to a bicycle path on your left. After viewing the sculpture, which is one of the largest bronze sculptures ever cast, follow the path to your left around a grassy area.

- 9.74 Cross the road and follow path to the Netherlands Carillon. The Carillon tower provides bell music performances May through September from 2 P.M. to 4 P.M. and from 6 P.M. to 8 P.M. June through August.

- 9.94 After viewing the Carillon, and possibly climbing the tower to meet the guest musician, follow the same path away from tower. Bear right when the path forks.

- 10.06 Turn right at the road and then immediately left toward roadway leading back to the bicycle path.

- 10.08 Turn right on main road away from sculpture.

- 10.29 Cross intersection and turn left back onto bicycle path leading to the cemetery entrance.

- 10.71 Leave the path and cross back over the road to the point where you began the Iwo Jima loop. Turn left toward the bridge and away from the cemetery.

- 10.95 Cross first bridge and bear right on the sidewalk around the traffic circle.

- 11.10 Cross the Arlington Memorial Bridge on the other side of the circle.

- 11.52 After the bridge, continue on the bicycle path toward the Lincoln Memorial.

- 11.79 Refreshments and bathrooms will be down on your right. The barriers and "No Traffic" signs are for cars only. Feel free to follow the wide road to your left to reach the front of the Lincoln Memorial. The top of the memorial's many steps provides a great view of the Washington Monument and the Capitol Building dome.

- 11.79 After viewing the memorial, face the reflecting pool and head to your right. Follow the sloping path away from the monument and along the 1.5-mile Reflecting Pool.

- 12.32 Cross the road and follow a wide path up to the Washington Monument. Follow the same path down the hill on the other side of the monument, where you'll find rest rooms and a refreshment/souvenir shop. From the souvenir shop, ride a short distance to your right to a traffic light. Turn left at the light to cross 15th and 14th Streets in quick succession. You will then be on one-way Jefferson Drive along the National Mall, where you'll pass the Smithsonian Castle (202) 357–2700, the National Air and Space Museum, the National Gallery of Art (202) 737–4215, and the Dept. of Agriculture.

- 13.76 Turn right on 1st St., and make a quick left on Maryland Ave. past the U.S. Botanical Gardens (202) 225–8333 on your right and a courtyard with small reflecting pool on your left.

- 13.97 A short distance later, cross the road to a path on your left leading up to the Capitol Building.

- 14.25 Turn left around the back of the Capitol and follow the path out to First St.

- 14.74 Turning left onto First street, the Library of Congress (202) 707–8000 will be on your right followed by the Supreme Court (202) 479–3030. Ride about half a mile toward Union Station.

- 15.16 Cross Columbus Circle toward Union Station bearing to the right along the service road, which then curves left directly in front of the station.

- 15.39 Turn left out of station and across E street.

- 15.46 Turn right on Louisiana Ave.

- 15.88 Bear right onto Constitution Ave. for two and a half blocks to Pennsylvania Ave.

- 16.11 Bear right on Pennsylvania Ave along the same route presidential inaugural parades have followed since the days of Thomas Jefferson. You will pass the Canadian Embassy and the National Archives (202) 501–5000 on your right, with the J. Edgar Hoover FBI building (202) 324–3447 on your left.

- 16.89 Turn right on 13th St. and then immediately left onto Pennsylvania. Freedom Plaza, which is often bustling with workers on break, planned activities, or kids riding bikes and skateboards, will be on your left. The National Theater and Willard Hotel are on the right.

- 17.17 You will reach a T intersection at 15th St. with a "Do Not Enter" sign directly in front of you. The sign doesn't apply to bicycles. Cross 15th straight past the sign and along the front steps of the U.S. Treasury Building.

- 17.25 Turn right through iron gates onto E. Executive Park path, which parallels the eastern side of the White House and leads to Pennsylvania Avenue.

- 17.41 Turn left on Pennsylvania Ave. to view the front of the White House. This section of Pennsylvania Ave. has been closed to cars but remains open for cyclists and pedestrians. On your left is Lafayette Square Park with lots of shady benches to rest your legs. Blair House and the Renwick Gallery will be on your right near the end of Pennsylvania Ave.

- 17.66 Pass by the automobile barriers and security hut before turning left on 17th St. Continue 3 blocks on 17th St. past the Corcoran Gallery of Art (202) 638–3211 and the Organization of American States building.

- 18.12 Cross Constitution Ave. and turn immediately right onto the path paralleling Constitution Ave.

- 18.65 Keep your eyes open for a road sign on your left indicating the intersection of 21st St. and Constitution Avenue. The sign will be near the road. At that intersection, turn left onto a path leading to the Vietnam Veterans Memorial (202) 634–1568. Dismount as you approach the memorial and walk your bike. On the other side of the memorial, walk to your left and then right to reach the road in front of the Lincoln Memorial.

- 18.93 Getting back on your bike, turn left in front of the memorial. Bear right around the memorial.
- 19.09 Take your second left turn, which will be away from the memorial toward the Ericsson Statue and bike path along the Potomac River.
- 19.18 Turn right onto the path and retrace the path back to the Thompson Boat Center.
- 20.34 Arrive back at the Thompson Boat Center parking lot. The Rock Creek Park Cruise also begins at the boat center and can be combined with the Monuments Ramble for a total ride of 36.5 miles. To follow the Park Cruise, continue north past the boat center parking lot and follow directions for Ride 19.

Rock Creek Park Cruise

Thompson Boat Center—Pierce Mill and Art Barn—
Rock Creek Park—Pierce Mill and Art Barn—
Thompson Boat Center

Rock Creek is a wandering little waterway making its shady way through the bustling urban center of the nation's capitol. Its gentle current meanders 22 miles from Laytonsville, MD, before flowing into Washington's Rock Creek Park, through a tree-filled valley, past the National Zoo, and finally joining the Potomac River just a few blocks from the White House. Its cool waters have brought vibrant wildlife to the city, including 35 species of fish, beavers, chipmunks, foxes, owls, hawks, and a variety of songbirds. And there's a good chance you'll spot some of those creatures as this ride takes you along the creek's banks and under some towering shade trees. You'll cross the creek five times over small bridges as you follow its winding path through the park, past the zoo, and to the spot of a restored 1780's wheat mill and barn.

The stone mill that once ground as many as 210 bushels of rye a day before closing in 1897 is now open year-round for public tours (202) 426–6908. The accompanying barn, now known as the Rock Creek Gallery or "Art Barn" (202) 244–2482, has been converted to a showplace for local artists, writers, and performers.

If no wildlife is spotted along the creek, you can always take one of the ride's two entrances to the National Zoo

---

(202) 673–4800, where you'll walk your bike among wild chee-tahs, chimpanzees, and 2,000 other animals.

Once past the zoo and mill, the ride leaves the creek to become a challenging, but shady, road climb through the north of the park.

You'll pass the park's Nature Center and Planetarium (202) 426–6829 with its guided nature walks and wildlife exhibits, as well as the park's horse center, where you can trade pedal power for horse power. Call (202) 362–0117 for horse rental rates and availability.

This 15.1-mile route can be shorted to 9.2 miles by skipping the uphill section, or lengthened to 35.5 miles by combining with the Washington Monuments Ramble (Ride 18).

A small detour, explained in the "Miles & Directions" section, will also take you into the heart of Georgetown's shopping and pub district.

The ride begins and ends at the Thompson Boat Center, where you can rent canoes to paddle the Potomac or end the day sipping drinks and watching boats from one of the adjacent Georgetown Waterfront's outdoor restaurants.

The Rock Creek Cruise is a combination of two routes in Michael Leccese's marvelous best-seller, *Short Bike Rides in and around Washington, D.C.* (The Globe Pequot Press, third edition, 1996).

The Basics

Start: Washington, D.C., at the Harry T. Thompson Boat Center near the intersection of Virginia Ave. and Rock Creek Potomac Parkway, NW. From Maryland or northern sections of the city, take the Parkway directly to the center parking lot. From the National Mall, follow Virginia Ave. to reach the center parking lot. Bicycles are rented from the boat center building, which is near the water behind and to the left of the parking lot.

Length: A little over 15 miles and can be combined, as noted below, with the Washington Monuments Ramble for a total of 35.5 miles.

Terrain: The ride is mostly rolling over gentle hills along wide bike paths. The 2.5-mile middle section, however, provides some fun and challenging climbs up twisting, shady roads. Numerous picnic areas along the climb provide ample rest if necessary. The route is mostly along paths and removed from traffic. This is a popular Washington area ride so be prepared for weekend crowds.

Food: Rest rooms are available at the boat center and at mile 4.26. Water is available at miles 4.26 and 8.09. Food can be found at the start of the ride at the boat center and along the Georgetown detour. The rest of the ride, however, is within the park and devoid of restaurants. Pack a lunch for one of the many shady picnic areas.

Miles & Directions

- 0.0 Turn left out of the Harry T. Thompson Boat Center parking lot onto the bike path paralleling Rock Creek Potomac Pkwy. You will be riding away from the Watergate and the Kennedy Center for the Performing Arts.
- .07 Bear right across the road at a fork in the path.
- .13 Stop at the stop sign and cross the road.
- .22 Again, note the stop sign before the crossing another road.

  Note: Turning left and up the hill will bring you to the Georgetown shopping and pub district. It's a good place to park your bike and stroll, sight-see, or eat up before your ride. Quick detours up the district's side streets will also reveal much of Georgetown's historic architecture. To make a quick tour of the shopping district, turn left and ride to the top of the hill, cross the road through the gas station parking lot, and turn left on M St. The M St. district continues for

N

Rock Creek

Beach Dr.

Oregon Ave.

Bingham Dr.

Joyce Rd.

Military Rd.

Ridge Rd.

Ross Dr.

Beach Dr.

Broad Branch Rd.

Tilden St.

Pierce Mill and Art Barn

Park Rd.

National
Zoological
Park

U.S. Naval
Observatory

Duke Ellington Memorial Bridge

Taft Bridge

Massachusetts Ave.

Rock Creek

Dupont Circle

Rock Creek Potomac Pkwy.

Francis Scott Key
Bridge

Potomac

Roosevelt
Island

River

START
Harry T. Thompson Boat Center

Virginia Ave.

about a mile. Retrace your steps to return to the Rock Creek Park Cruise.

- .74   Continue straight on the path across two roads.
- 1.09   Path veers to your right crossing the first of five bridges over Rock Creek.
- 1.10   Turn left after the bridge.
- 1.84   Bear left over the second bridge and continue up a short, steep climb.
- 2.05   At the top of the hill, dismount and walk across Rock Creek Pkwy. to the bike path on your right. (This is a busy intersection so be patient and use caution when crossing.)
- 2.30   Dismount and walk your bike over the bridge's narrow sidewalk.
- 2.32   Turn left along the path immediately before the tunnel. (This section of the path closes during the evening. Read the entrance sign for closing times.)
- 2.59   You'll reach the first of the ride's two zoo enhances. Cycling is prohibited in the zoo, but you may dismount and walk your bike around the 163-acre complex. To enter the zoo turn left and follow the signs noting various attractions. To continue the ride, cross the road and continue on the bicycle path.
- 2.81   Leave the gated portion of the path.
- 2.98   Your second chance to enter the zoo.
- 3.55   Cross a third bridge to your left.
- 3.88   Cross your fourth bridge, turning left on the other side.
- 4.19   Cross to your left over a fifth bridge leading to a sunny, grassy area with picnic tables, rest rooms, and a water fountain. You are one-quarter of the way through the ride so this is a good spot to refill your water bottle or take break.
- 4.26   A water fountain will be on your left. A covered picnic area with a wood-burning grill and rest rooms is directly across the field from the water fountain.

- 4.36 A pleasant waterfall will be on your right, with the Pierce Mill and Art Barn to your left.
- 4.40 Turn left into the parking lot to visit the Barn or Mill. When ready to resume, continue straight along the path.
- 4.61 Path continues through a picnic area parking lot.
  Note: To skip the challenging 2-mile uphill section simply turn around and follow the path back to the boat house for a total ride of 9.2 miles.
- 4.68 After the parking lot, cross the road to a path leading to your left. Leave the path and turn right for a challenging up-hill climb.
- 5.49 Bear left at a fork in the road marked with a sign for the Rock Creek Park Nature Center.
- 6.0 Bear right at a second fork. You will ride downhill past signs marking the entrance to the riding stables and nature area.
- 6.50 You'll reach the Military Road intersection with a traffic light. Cross the road and continue on the path to your right.
- 6.55 Pass entrance to Fort De Russy Memorial, where a strate-gically located cannon helped defend the city from a July, 1864 Confederate attack. To reach the site, walk your bike 200 yards along a small path to your right.
  Note: The next half mile is fast and fun. But the trail is narrow and lined with trees, so be careful not to lose control.
- 6.49 Cross a small road and continue straight on the path.
- 7.18 Leave the path and turn right on unmarked Bingham Dr.
- 7.65 Turn right at your first intersection onto the Beach Dr. path.
- 8.09 A water fountain will be along the path on your right. You're about halfway through the ride with some steep climbs ahead, so now would be a good time for a drink.
- 8.40 Leave the path and turn right onto Joyce Rd.

- 8.50 Follow the road curving to the left and up a steep hill along Ross Dr.
- 9.64 Bear left at T intersection away from the Nature Center sign.
- 10.39 Turn left onto Branch Rd. and immediately right into the picnic area parking lot. The parking lot leads back to the path, Mill, and Art Barn.
- 10.70 You will arrive at the Mill and Art Barn parking lot with the waterfall down and to your left. Follow the path back to the Thompson Boat Center parking lot.
- 15.10 Arrive at the boat center parking lot. To combine this route with the "Washington Monuments Ramble" (Ride 18), for a total length of 35.5 miles, continue south past the boat center and pick up the directions at mile 0.0 of the Monuments Ramble.

20

Washington Bridges Ramble

Harry T. Thompson Boat Center—Francis Scott Key Bridge—Arlington Memorial Bridge—Inlet Bridge— Outlet Bridge—Kurtz Bridge—George Mason Memorial Bridge—Francis Scott Key Bridge—Harry T. Thompson Boat Center

Bring your camera!

The Washington Bridges Ramble is a fun way to beat the heat and to snap some of Washington's most picturesque photos. Unlike the Monuments ride, which provides an up-close look at the monuments and their history, the Bridges Ramble takes a broader perspective, presenting the beauty of those buildings and their natural surroundings through a series of long-range views.

The ride follows the banks of the Potomac River and the Tidal Basin, providing elevated and unobstructed views from the area's numerous stone bridges. And because a steady breeze blows in off the Potomac River, riders enjoy a rare escape from the city's notorious heat and humidity. (The effect even worked in the dog days of August when this ride was verified.)

The ride begins at the Harry T. Thompson Boat Center (202) 333–4861 and travels west a short distance through the heart of Georgetown before crossing the Chesapeake and Ohio Canal and the Potomac River along the towering Francis Scott

155

Key Bridge. The bridge provides a great view of the Kennedy Center and the Watergate.

Riders will then cross into Virginia on the other side of the bridge and follow the river along a wide, paved path to the Arlington Memorial Bridge. This unique bridge features stone and bronze sculptures on each end and attractive stone column railings. From this vantage point you'll have an excellent view of the Lincoln Memorial, the Washington Monument, and the distant National Cathedral.

You'll then cross the tiny, stone Inlet Bridge, where the Potomac River flows into the Tidal Basin. This bridge provides a view of the Tidal Basin's thousands of cherry trees, which bloom each April and are the subject of the annual Cherry Blossom Festival (202) 619–7222.

Continuing around the Tidal Basin, you'll cross the Outlet Bridge, which spans the Washington Channel's entrance into the basin before reaching the small Kurtz Bridge. The Kurtz Bridge is on the far end of the basin and provides one of the city's best views of the Jefferson Memorial.

The ride again crosses the Potomac over the George Mason Memorial Bridge and follows the water back to the Key Bridge and the Thompson Boat Center.

This ride can be combined with the Monuments Ramble at numerous points along the route. The areas where the two rides intersect are noted in the Miles & Directions section.

This Ramble has only one climb and is largely removed from traffic. It is a good route for families or those looking for easy ride.

The Basics

Start: Washington, D.C., at the Harry T. Thompson Boat Center near the intersection of Virginia Ave. and Rock Creek Potomac Parkway, NW. From Maryland or northern sections of the city, take the Parkway directly to the center parking lot. From the National Mall, follow Virginia Ave. to reach the center parking lot.

Bicycles are rented from the boat-center building, which is near the water behind and to the left of the parking lot.

Length: 11.5 miles.

Terrain: Very easy ride. The ride has only one, short climb and is mainly along bicycle paths with no traffic.

Food: A single water bottle and an apple brought along on this ride should do the trick, but water is available at the ride's beginning and end as well as at miles 3.7, 4.5, 5.8, and 7.0. Rest rooms are available at the beginning and end as well as at miles 3.7 and 6.5.

Miles & Directions

- 0.0   Turn right in the boat center parking lot across a small bridge toward the Potomac River and the boat center building.
- .07   Turn right at the water toward the Georgetown Waterfront Complex. (Careful as you navigate `a 20-foot unpaved section.)

  Note: The Georgetown Waterfront is a lively area of outdoor restaurants and shops that is often buzzing on warm afternoons with boats and people watchers. It's a good place to fuel up before your ride and to relax afterward.
- .24   Turn right away from the water to leave the Georgetown Waterfront.
- .30   Turn left onto K St. You will be under a large overpass.
- .38   Turn right onto unmarked Wisconsin Ave. You'll turn directly across from the "Harbor Parking" lot and begin a small—and the only—climb of the ride.
- .50   Cross a small bridge over the Chesapeake & Ohio Canal. The canal features an adjacent, unpaved path and has become a popular recreational and commuting route.
- .55   Turn left at the traffic light onto M St. (The Neighborhoods Ramble crosses this intersection at mile 4.67 of that ride.)

  Note: You are now in the heart of Georgetown's shopping district. Feel free to lock your bike to one of the street signs and tour this

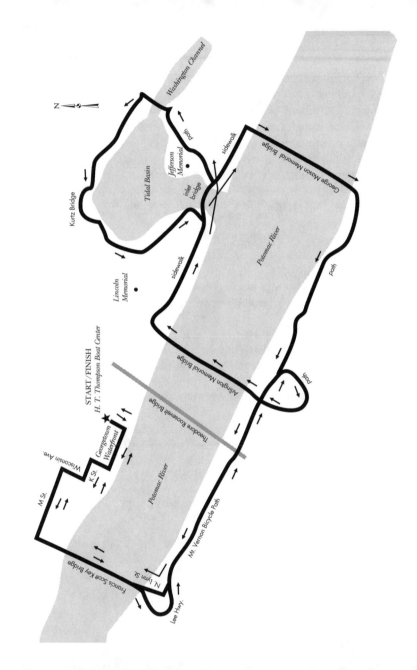

N

START/FINISH
H. T. Thompson Boat Center
Georgetown Waterfront
Wisconsin Ave.
M. St.
K. St.
Francis Scott Key Bridge
N. Lynn St.
Lee Hwy.
Mt. Vernon Bicycle Path
Theodore Roosevelt Bridge
Arlington Memorial Bridge
Potomac River
Path
George Mason Memorial Bridge
Potomac River
sidewalk
inlet bridge
Jefferson Memorial
Tidal Basin
sidewalk
Path
Washington Channel
Kurtz Bridge
Lincoln Memorial
Path

nationally recognized section of the nation's capitol. You'll also pass this way during the ride's return leg.

- .69   Continue straight through the traffic light at Potomac St.
- .75   Continue straight through the traffic light at 33rd St.
- .84   Continue through the traffic light at 34th St.
- .89   Ride to the crosswalk on the other side of this intersection and turn left toward the Francis Scott Key Bridge.
- .92   On the sidewalk, cross the 0.4-mile Francis Scott Key Bridge.

   Note: This is one of the ride's three larger bridges and offers an excellent view of the Kennedy Center for the Performing Arts, the infamous Watergate complex (both on your left), the C & O Canal, and the Potomac River.

- 1.3   After the bridge at the traffic light, bear a few feet to your right and continue on the sidewalk across the unmarked road.
- 1.4   Turn left (without crossing the intersection) along the sidewalk at Lee Highway.
- 1.5   Cross N. Lynn street and continue on the paved but unmarked Mt. Vernon bicycle path.

   Note: The town of Rossyln is on your right. Rossyln, a growing Washington suburb, is home to USA Today *and a growing technology industry.*

- 1.7   Bear left across the overpass. (Check out the view before the overpass veers down and to the right.)
- 2.0   Pass the entrance to Theodore Roosevelt Island. The island prohibits bicycles but it is a great place to explore on foot or have a shady picnic lunch.
- 2.1   Bear left onto a boardwalk-like section of the bicycle path.
- 2.3   Ride under the Theodore Roosevelt Memorial Bridge.
- 2.8   Continue straight under the Arlington Memorial Bridge.
- 3.0   Turn right and follow the path across an unmarked road. Trail will bear right after the road.

Note: To visit the Arlington Memorial Cemetery, see mile 8.31 of the Washington Monuments Ramble.

- 3.2   Use caution as you cross a second road and continue on the path to the Arlington Memorial Bridge.
- 3.3   Note the large stone eagles and stone column railings as you cross this 0.4-mile bridge.

  Note: You can see the National Cathedral to the far left, as well as the Lincoln Memorial straight ahead and the Washington Monument a little to the right.

- 3.7   Note the two large, bronze statues of man, woman, and child as the bridge ends.
- 3.7+ Follow the sidewalk to the right and across two small roads.

  Note: You are now beside the Lincoln Memorial and at the corner of the National Mall and the city's monument district. The National Reflecting Pool is ahead and to your left with the Vietnam Memorial a little left of the pool. The Washington Monument is about 0.5 mile straight ahead. Feel free to take time to explore this area. (See mile 11.79 of the Washington Monuments Ramble for an extensive tour of the National Mall.)

- 3.8   Turn right on the sidewalk toward the Potomac River. Use caution as you cross two small intersections. The Ericsson Statue will be on your right.
- 4.0   Turn left onto the path by the water. This is a very shaded, cool area to ride.

  Note: Turn left at mile 4.2 to visit the Franklin Delano Roosevelt Memorial Park. The park features a visitors center and rest rooms. After turning right into the park, walk your bike through the exhibits. Follow the path on the other side of the park and continue the ride from mileage direction 4.7+. (See mile 1.52 of the Monuments Ramble for more information about the FDR Memorial.)

- 4.5   You'll pass a water fountain on your right.
- 4.7   Veer left across the unmarked road immediately before the small Inlet Bridge.

- 4.7+ Turn right (left if you are coming from the memorial) across the Inlet Bridge.
  Note: This bridge offers a picture-perfect view of the Tidal Basin, Jefferson Memorial, and the Washington Monument.
- 5.3 Bear left to follow the path down and along the water. Continue following path around the Jefferson Memorial.
- 5.4 Continue on the bicycle path around the Tidal Basin.
- 5.5 Bear left across the Outlet Bridge and continue along the water.
- 5.8 You'll reach the Tidal Basin Boat House (202) 479–2426 on your left, which rents pedal boats by the hour. ($7 for a two-seater, $14 for a four-seater). A refreshment stand with drinks, hot dogs, and snacks will be on your right.
- 5.8 Continue along the path past the boat house.
- 6.0 Turn left on the path over the Kurtz Bridge.
  Note: This bridge offers one of the city's best views of the Jefferson Memorial.
- 6.1 Bear left after the bridge along the path toward the water.
- 6.5 You'll reach a side entrance to the FDR Memorial. Rest rooms and a visitors center will be up the stairs and to your right.
- 6.8 Turn left to cross the Inlet Bridge.
- 6.9 Do not bear left along the water as you did earlier, but continue straight along the outer sidewalk.
- 7.0 You'll reach a refreshment stand on your left. Turn right across the road and follow the path uphill to the George Mason Memorial Bridge.
- 7.1 Begin the trip across this 0.4-mile bridge, known locally as the 14th Street Bridge.
- 7.5 Bear right along the path after the bridge.
- 7.6 Turn left at a T intersection in the path.
- 7.7 Cross a small bridge.

- 7.8 After the bridge, bear right on the path toward the water.
- 7.9 You'll pass the Navy and Marine Memorial on your left.
- 8.8 Ride under the Arlington Memorial Bridge.
- 9.2 Cross a small path bridge.
- 9.7 Pass the entrance to Theadore Roosevelt Island. (Remember—no bicycles allowed.)
- 9.8 Ride up and over the highway overpass.
- 10.1 Turn right at the traffic light onto the sidewalk beside N. Lynn St.
- 10.1+ Cross a small road and follow the sidewalk to the Francis Scott Key Bridge.
  Note: Use caution at mile 11.7 along the bridge as cars turn right here as an alternative bridge exit.
- 10.5 Turn right on the sidewalk after the bridge. At the 34th St. traffic light, veer back onto M St. and continue straight. You are again in the heart of Georgetown's shopping and restaurant district.
- 10.8 Turn right at the traffic light onto Wisconsin Ave.
- 10.9 Cross a small bridge over the C & O Canal. (Careful to control your speed as you approach the stop sign at the bottom of this hill.)
- 11.0 Turn left at the stop sign onto Water St. (If you have knobby tires, you can also return to the boat center by crossing Water St. and turning left onto a dirt and stone path by the water back to the Georgetown Waterfront).
- 11.1 Turn right back into the Georgetown Waterfront.
- 11.1+ Turn left along the water and ride along the Georgetown Waterfront.
- 11.3 Turn left at the boat center.
- 11.4 Cross a small bridge back into the parking lot.
- 11.5 Arrive back at the boat center parking lot. (The Rock Creek Park Cruise and Washington Monuments Ramble also begin and end here.)

21

Washington, D.C. Neighborhoods Ramble

Adams Morgan—Kalorama—Georgetown—Dupont Circle—Logan Circle—U Street—Meridian Hill—Woodley Park—Adams Morgan

Washington, D.C., is the cornerstone of American democracy and a hub of international politics. World leaders stroll its avenues while taxes, laws, and wars are decided within its grand old structures. Each year, thousands flock to Washington's historic sites and to see their government and elected officials at work. It's a city that belongs to all Americans.

But it's also home to more than a million full-time Washingtonians. People who live, work, and play among the monuments and memorials. It's home to small community parks and distinctive, close-knit neighborhoods. Residents walk quiet side streets, shop at the corner store, and eat at mom and pop restaurants. Wealth and poverty, along with an eclectic blend of cultures, live side-by-side to form a unique city character not mentioned on the official monuments map.

This ride will steer you away from that map to show you the many sides of unofficial Washington. You'll pedal past the mansions of Kalorama, which sit beside international embassies. You'll tour the quaint village architecture of historic Georgetown and sit under the shade trees of some of Washington's dozens of neighborhood parks. Meridian Hill Park, for example, tucked away in the Mt. Pleasant neighborhood, is a city treasure with a 70-foot cascading fountain surrounded by majestic stone steps.

Urban sights and sounds will surround you as you ride through the Logan Circle neighborhood and the funky shops and restaurants of the "U St. Corridor" and Adams Morgan. Small locally owned restaurants featuring everything from Caribbean to Ethiopian are hidden along the route.

The ride also passes by a few of the more traditional attractions, such as the National Zoo (202) 673–4800, Georgetown University (202) 687–0100, and the towering French Embassy.

The ride starts in the center of the eclectic Adams Morgan neighborhood with its ethnically diverse residents, music, and shops. You'll then pass the much photographed Marilyn Monroe mural marking the Woodley Park neighborhood before crossing the second of two 80-foot-high bridges with long views of natural Washington. The ride continues downhill past Kalorama's mansions and embassies and by the small shops and historically preserved townhomes of Georgetown.

After a rest at Dupont Circle, considered one of the hubs of residential and commercial Washington, you'll ride through urban Logan Circle and U St. Both neighborhoods are safe during the day, but some caution should be used when making your way through these areas.

After a challenging climb to the top of 16th St., you can rest by the flowing waters of Meridian Hill Park before making your way past the National Zoo and back to Adams Morgan.

For more information about the neighborhoods or sites along the ride, call the Historical Society of Washington, D.C. at (202) 785–2068 or the Washington, D.C. Convention and Visitor's Association at (202) 789–7000.

The Basics

Start: Washington, D.C., 2417 18th St., public parking lot. Check with the parking attendant for rates. To get to the lot from the north, take Connecticut Ave. south to Calvert St. Turn left on Calvert St. Cross the bridge and continue for about half a mile. The parking lot will be on your left about 200 yards past Columbia Rd. From the south, take Connecticut Ave. north. Bear right as the road forks near the Washington Hilton Hotel. You'll be on Columbia Rd. Follow Columbia Rd. to 18th St. Turn right. The parking lot will be on your left about 200 yards down the hill.

Length: 13.25 miles.

Terrain: Though short, this ride can be very challenging. Some sections involve long, steep climbs while other areas include urban traffic. Heavily trafficked areas should be ridden with caution and can be unnerving for those unaccustomed to urban cycling. When appropriate, the ride's directions include sidewalk detours. The ride also includes places to rest before and after the steepest hills.

Food: Food abounds along much of the ride. Adams Morgan, Georgetown (mile 4.5), U St. (mile 8.4) and Cleveland Park (mile 11.2) are all home to restaurants and stores with rest rooms and refreshments. Many of the parks also provide water fountains.

Miles & Directions

- 0.0   Turn right out of the parking lot onto 18th St. You'll pass funky restaurants and shops as you ride this section of the Adams Morgan neighborhood.
- .13   Continue straight through the traffic light at the Columbia Rd./18th St. intersection. 18th St. will become Calvert St. as it curves to the left.
- .41   Follow Calvert St. through a second traffic light toward the bridge. You may want to ride on the wide bridge sidewalk, which provides a safer crossing and better view.
- .58   Leave the bridge and continue on the sidewalk to Connecticut Ave. The Monroe mural will be on the side of a building up and to your right.
- .64   Cross Connecticut Ave. before turning left to follow the Connecticut Ave. sidewalk over a second 80-foot-high bridge.

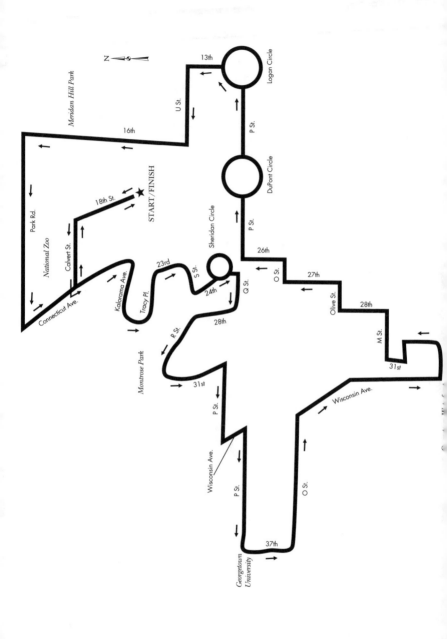

13th

Logan Circle

N

Meridian Hill Park

U St.

16th

P St.

DuPont Circle

Park Rd.

START/FINISH

18th St.

Sheridan Circle

P St.

National Zoo

Calvert St.

23rd

S St.

26th

O St.

27th

Kalorama Ave.

Tracy Pl.

24th

Q St.

Olive St.

28th

Connecticut Ave.

28th

M St.

R St.

31st

Montrose Park

Wisconsin Ave.

31st

P St.

Wisconsin Ave.

P St.

O St.

37th

Georgetown University

- .73   Cross the bridge.
- .99   Leave the bridge, get back on the road, and bear right at the circle.
- 1.07 Turn right at the T intersection onto an unmarked road. The Chinese Embassy will be on your right and the Algerian Embassy straight ahead as you turn.
- 1.13 Pass the Portuguese Embassy followed by the towering mansion and grand architecture of the French Embassy.
- 1.18 Turn right at the T intersection of 23rd St. and Kalorama Rd. The road curves gently down hill past some of the city's largest homes.
- 1.47 Turn left at the T intersection of Tracy Pl. and Kalorama Rd.
- 1.74 Turn right on 23rd St.
- 1.89 Turn right onto S St. at the T intersection. The S St. sign is hidden by a tree on the right.
- 1.99 Turn left onto 24th St., where you will immediately reach a T intersection with Massachusetts Ave.
- 2.04 Turn left on Massachusetts Ave.
- 2.15 Bear right around the traffic circle to 23rd St.
- 2.20 Turn right onto 23rd St.
- 2.26 Turn right onto the Q St. sidewalk. Cross a small bridge along the narrow sidewalk. You'll be able to see the top of the Washington Monument to the right.
  Note: After leaving the bridge you may want to continue on the wide, red brick sidewalk as the road is narrow and without a shoulder. But if you feel comfortable, ride on the road.
- 2.24 You will reach the historic Dumbarton House mansion and grounds (202) 337–2288, which are open for public tours.
- 2.26 Turn right on 28th St. for a short uphill climb.
- 2.81 Bear left at the top of the hill.

- 2.93 You will reach the entrance to the Oak Hill Cemetery. The cemetery, open to the public, is known for its rolling hills and unique headstones.

- 3.02 You'll reach shady Montrose Park, which is a great place to take a drink and rest after your long climb.

- 3.14 Here you'll find the main entrance to a second historic mansion and gardens, Dumbarton Oaks (202) 339–6400. Take a few moments to stroll the grand estate.

- 3.14 To skip the estate, turn left at the entrance onto unmarked 31st St. (The estate entrance is at the 31st St. intersection, so if you tour the grounds, exit straight down unmarked 31st St.)

- 3.26 You'll pass one of Georgetown's most historic estates, the Tudor House (202) 965–0400 on your right. The estate and its walkways are open to the public. For more information about any of Georgetown's historic sites, call Janice Artemel at the Georgetown Heritage Trust (202) 338–6222, which helped design this section of the ride.

- 3.43 Turn right onto P St.

- 3.58 Turn left at the traffic light of the unmarked T intersection. Then make an immediate right onto a other section of P St. (You may want to ride on the sidewalk for a few blocks as this section of P St. is made of uneven, stone bricks.)

- 4.06 Follow the roadway as it veers left.

- 4.13 The Georgetown University entrance will be on your right. Feel free to dismount and walk your bike around the historic campus. An information booth with maps will be on your left as you enter.

- 4.13 To skip the university turn left onto O St. at the campus entrance. Or, or after touring the GU grounds, continue straight down O St. after exiting.

- 4.57 Turn right onto Wisconsin Ave. Use caution as this is one of the more heavily trafficked sections of the ride.

- 4.67 You'll reach the Wisconsin Ave./M St. intersection, which is the heart of the Georgetown shopping and pub district. Feel free to lock your bike and stroll the wide sidewalks, which offer a mix of national stores and mom and pop outlets.
- 4.67 Cross M St. and continue down the hill.
- 4.97 Cross Water St. and bear left onto the path by the Potomac River. This path is short but covered with small stones so those with skinny tires may want to walk their bikes. Note the Kennedy Center for the Performing Arts to your left as you look out over the water.
- 5.08 Leave the stone pathway for a smooth brick path that is part of the Georgetown Waterfront. The waterfront, with its outdoor pubs and docked boats, is usually crowded and festive each evening and weekend of the warm season.

    Note: You are about halfway through the ride, so the waterfront may be a good spot to have some lunch and rest up before continuing.
- 5.20 Turn left at the large stone sundial, which marks the end of the Georgetown Waterfront.

    Note: If you continue on the stone-filled path along the water you will reach the Thompson Boat Center, which, in addition to renting canoes, kayaks and bicycles, is the start/finish point for both the Washington Monuments Ramble and the Rock Creek Park Cruise.
- 5.31 Turn left at the stop sign onto an unmarked road under a large overpass.
- 5.31 Take your first right turn which will be across from the waterfront entrance.
- 5.49 You'll cross the Chesapeake & Ohio Canal. The canal has a pleasant, paved path along its waters leading away from the city. Check out the C & O Visitors Center to your right for a map of the canal bicycle path.
- 5.55 Turn right onto M St. Once again, be cautious of heavy traffic. Continue straight on M St. for about a quarter mile

until you reach the crosswalk and traffic light directly in front of the Four Seasons Hotel.

- 5.71 Turn left across M St. onto 28th St.
- 5.80 Turn right onto unmarked Olive St.
- 5.87 Bear left as Olive turns into 27th St. near one of George-town's neighborhood parks.
- 6.04 Turn right onto O St. near the tennis courts.
- 6.10 Bear left as O St. becomes 26th St.
- 6.15 Turn right onto P. St. near the softball field. Continue on P St. for about half a mile, past shops and restaurants to Dupont Circle.
- 6.71 You'll arrive at Dupont Circle, which is one of Washington's liveliest areas and busiest residential hubs. A dense mix of residential and commercial buildings line the streets surrounding the circle park and fountain. Connecticut Ave.—one of the city's main thoroughfares—also runs down the middle of the neighborhood.
- 6.71 As you approach the circle intersection, hop onto the sidewalk to your right near the CVS Drug Store. It will be easier to make your way around the circle along the sidewalk and crosswalks. Turn right along the sidewalk at the light in front of the circle. Follow the sidewalk as it curves around to the left.
- 6.82 You'll reach a pedestrian island with a light post and the second of two signs for 1300 Connecticut Ave. Turn left to cross the two roads circling the park and enter the circle toward the fountain. Sit by the fountain and enjoy the cool, moist breeze.
- 6.87 Turn right directly before the fountain to follow your first path out of the circle.
- 6.90 Cross the road to a second pedestrian island. Turn left and make an immediate right onto P St.
- 7.17 Cross 17th St. A CVS Drug Store will be on your left where you can stock up on water and snacks.

- 7.27 Cross 16th St. with the Carnegie Institution of Washington on your right.
- 7.52 Shortly after 14th St., you'll see Washington's nationally recognized Studio Theatre on your left.
  Note: The next few miles take on a more urban, gritty character. You'll read graffiti, hear loud music and construction, and most likely see some folks hanging out in front of various stores. It is the way of city life. This section of the ride is safe when ridden during the day, but use common sense and caution.
- 7.59 As you reach the Logan Circle intersection traffic light, cross to the left-hand sidewalk rather than going through the light or around the circle. Follow the sidewalk as it eventually curves left away from the circle and onto 13th St. When traffic lightens, leave the sidewalk and continue straight on 13th St.
- 8.14 Turn left onto U St. This area is known as the "U St. Corridor" and has been the subject of enormous revitalization over the last decade. The corridor, near Howard University, is home to many funky shops and restaurants.
- 8.53 Turn right onto 16th St. (Make sure you turn onto 16th St. and not New Hampshire Ave., which is immediately in front of 16th.) This turn begins a long climb to the top of 16th St. and the entrance to Meridian Hill Park at the intersection with Euclid St.
- 8.96 You'll reach the 16th St./Euclid St. intersection. A park entrance will be on your right. Enter the park and ride back to the top of a gorgeous cascading waterfall with stone steps lining each side. If you are willing to ride back up 16th street, walk down the stone steps to enjoy the cool air and shady resting spots. (At the bottom of the fountain turn right to get back to 6th Street. Turn right on 16th St. and ride back up the hill.)
- 8.96 Continue straight through the 16th St./Euclid St. intersection.
- 9.19 Continue straight through the 16th St./Columbia Rd. intersection.

- 9.54 Turn left onto Park Rd.
- 10.07 After crossing two intersections, bear right to stay on Park Rd. Enjoy this downhill section—the ride's toughest climb is just ahead.
- 10.21 Bear left over the bridge.
- 10.69 Continue straight through the traffic light and over another bridge. Note the waterfall on your right.
  Note: The Pierce Mill and Art Barn mentioned in the Rock Creek Park Cruise will be on your right immediately after the bridge. Consult the Cruise guide for information about the Barn and Mill.
- 10.69 Continue straight up the hill. The ride's most difficult climb begins here.
- 11.11 Congratulations—you have reached the end of the climb and the remainder of the ride is mostly downhill.
- 11.27 Turn left onto Connecticut Ave. This is the Cleveland Park section of Washington.
- 12.14 The National Zoo (202) 673–4800 entrance will be on your left at the traffic light. The 2,000+ animal zoo is open until 8 P.M. in the spring and summer and 6 P.M. in the fall and winter. Cycling is prohibited in the zoo but feel free to dismount and walk among the cheetahs and chimpanzees. After touring the zoo return to Connecticut Ave. and turn left.
- 12.14 Continue straight on Connecticut Ave. past the zoo entrance. You are now in the Woodley Park neighborhood.
- 12.62 Turn left onto Calvert St. toward the ride's first bridge. Again, a wide sidewalk provides a better view and safe crossing.
- 13.13 You'll reach the Calvert St./Columbia Rd. intersection where Calvert becomes 18 St. Continue straight through the intersection onto 18th St.
- 13.25 You've finished the ride. The parking lot will be on your left.

West Virginia

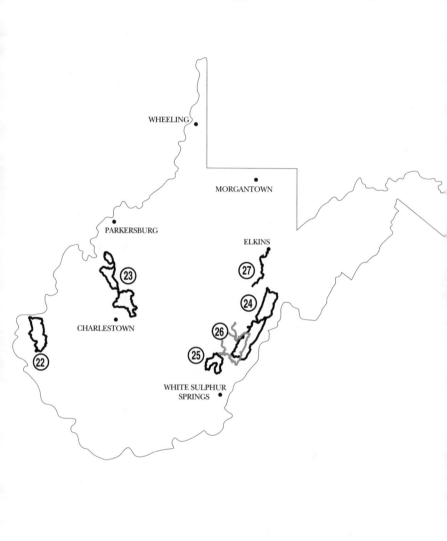

WHEELING •

MORGANTOWN •

PARKERSBURG •

ELKINS •

㉗

㉓

㉔

CHARLESTOWN •

㉖

㉕

㉒

WHITE SULPHUR
SPRINGS •

West Virginia

22

Milton Getaway Challenge

Milton—Dudley Gap—Ona—Balls Gap—Milton

If you're hankering for some real hill climbing and the cure for too much civilization, this loop will exercise your granny gear and quest for solitude, along with providing lovely views of West Virginia's rows of forested ridges. The westernmost ride in this book, this route through Cabell County is a true challenge, despite its moderate length of 42 miles. A favorite of the Mountain State Wheelers Bicycle Club, it was contributed and verified by Jim Saulters of St. Albans, West Virginia.

At the start in Milton, you can take a public tour of Blenko Glass, famous for its hand-blown commemorative glassware. And 17.6 miles into the ride, you can make a 0.5-mile detour to Ona Speedway, the only paved oval track in West Virginia, and a small country airport that offers rides in private planes. But outside of Milton and the town of Ona halfway through the ride, the route follows backroads in the Mountain State so isolated and so lightly traveled that you will not run across so much as a picnic ground. Accommodations are available in both towns, however. Milton features the Wine Cellar Bed and Breakfast (301–743–5665) while Ona offers the Foxfire Camp Grounds (304–743–5622), allowing you to turn this challenge into a two-day cruise. Despite the solitude, all the roads are paved.

The Basics

Start: Milton, at the Little League fields on County Fair Rd. To get to the ride's start, take the Milton exit (exit 28) off I–64; drive

0.3 mile south; turn right (west) at the traffic light onto Rte. 60; and drive 0.4 mile into downtown Milton. Drive through the second traffic light another 0.4 mile to the Milton Junior High School. Park in the school parking lot.

Length: 42 miles.

Terrain: Hilly, no doubt about it. Traffic is normally light, except for around Milton and Ona.

Food: Convenience stores and fast-food restaurants in Milton and halfway through the ride at Ona; no other services along the route. Carry snacks, water, and tools.

Miles & Directions

Note: Follow directions carefully, as not every small street is shown on the map.

- 0.0   Turn right (east) onto Rte. 60. At 0.4 mile you can stock up on snacks at the Chevron convenience store on your right. At the traffic light turn left onto Smith St.
- 0.6   Turn right at the stop sign onto Mason St.
- 0.65 Turn left onto Rte. 15 (Glenwood St.). At the stop sign at mile 0.9, continue straight under I–64.
- 4.4   Turn right onto Rte. 9 (Dudley Gap Rd.). In 0.75 mile, you'll begin a long climb up to Dudley Gap. "Hope you brought your granny!" notes Jim Saulters.
- 6.2   Turn left onto Rte. 11 (Barkers Ridge Rd.), which rolls and weaves in a wonderful rollercoaster ride, offering lovely views of the forested ridges. At mile 9.0, bear right at the unmarked Y intersection to stay on Rte. 11. At miles 11.0 and 11.7, you'll pass some television towers on your right.
- 12.5 Continue straight onto Rte. 1 (Union Ridge Rd.), which intersects from your right.
- 12.6 Bear left (south) to stay on Rte. 1; stay on the ridge, *not* taking the obvious downhill to the right (which is Big Seven Rd.). In 0.25 mile you'll begin a long, pleasurable, winding

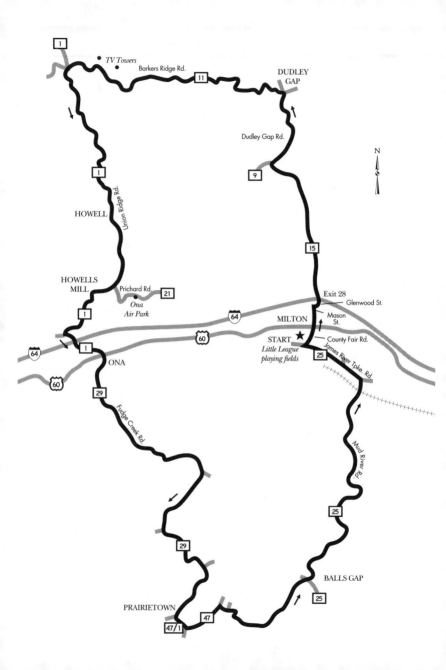

downhill. At mile 15.0, bear right at the unmarked Y intersection to stay on Rte. 1.

- 18.0 Bear to the right to stay on Rte. 1, where Rte. 21 (Prichard Rd.) comes in from the left. If, however, you'd like a nice 0.5-mile detour and maybe take a ride in a private plane, turn left onto Rte. 21 to visit the Ona Speedway. Then return to this spot to continue the ride. At mile 18.6 cross the Mud River at Howells Mill. At mile 19.9, you'll pass underneath I–64.

- 20.8 Here you can refuel at the Exxon convenience store where Rte. 1 ends at Rte. 60. Then continue straight across the intersection onto Rte. 29. At 24.2, bear right to stay on Rte. 29. At mile 26.2, bear left at the Y intersection, following the sign to Salt Rock. At mile 26.5, you'll climb up to the top of a ridge; on the downhill use caution on the steep switchbacks.

- 29.0 Turn left at the T intersection onto unmarked Rte. 47/1 in the unmarked community of Prairietown. In 0.3 mile turn left onto Rte. 47, following the signs to Milton and Balls Gap. In 1.2 miles you'll grind up a steep hill, followed by a slightly less steep descent.

- 33.0 Turn left onto Rte. 25 (Mud River Rd.) and ride over the top of Balls Gap, marked by a church on your right. Watch your speed on the left-hand sweeper on the other side!

- 35.8 Before crossing the Mud River, turn left at Zoar Baptist Church onto Rte. 25/12 (W. Mud River Rd.).

- 40.3 After passing under a railroad trestle, turn left onto Rte. 25 (James River Tpke. Rd.). At mile 41.0 pass the warehouse for Supervalu Food Distributors.

- 41.2 Bear right at Blenko Glass onto County Fair Rd.

- 41.4 Arrive back at your car.

- 41.6 Turn left at the Chevron gas station onto Rte. 60.

- 42.0 Arrive back at Milton Junior High School.

23

Sternwheel Regatta Century Classic

*Elkview—Sissonville—Liberty—Given—Fairplain—
Sissonville—Elkview*

This 100-mile ride north of Charleston takes you on a challenging tour through Kanawha, Putnam, and Jackson counties in western central West Virginia. You will climb forested ridges to behold panoramic vistas, soar down slopes into a river valley, and cycle through cultivated farmland. You may choose to picnic at the top of Allen Fork Road where it intersects with Route 34 about 35 miles into the ride and then take a tour of Fisher Ridge Winery a few miles later.

The ride's unusual name originated from the Sternwheel Regatta, a festival that started in Charleston on Labor Day in 1970 and whose highlight is a boat race among sternwheel riverboats. Over the years the Sternwheel Regatta has grown to a celebration ten days long that attracts more than 100,000 spectators for the events and concerts, all of which are free. In 1979 the Mountain State Wheelers Bicycle Club was asked to organize a bike ride for the festival; now the challenging ride attracts some 400 cyclists each year. "You can mention that if riders do the Regatta bike ride the last weekend in August during the festival, they will enjoy full support, which includes sag wagons, food, water,

STERNWHEEL REGATTA CENTURY CLASSIC

security and emergency services, and a dinner the night before the ride," notes Dennis A. Strawn of Charleston, West Virginia, who contributed and verified the map and cue sheet.

Although the Sternwheel Regatta classic was originally conceived as a one-day century ride, you can modify it in several ways. Because the 103-mile ride is three successive loops, it can be shortened to a 42-mile challenge or an 83-mile classic by returning after only the first or second loop. Alternatively, the ride can be turned into a two-day weekend by staying overnight at the Wildwood Campground (304–372–2436) at Staats Mill, 6 miles from Fairplain, about 70 miles into the ride.

Like most locales isolated enough to be ideal for road riding in West Virginia, here, too, places to get food are few and far between. There are a few convenience stores, but load up on snacks, water, and tools—unless, of course, you join the riders with sag support at the actual Sternwheel Regatta!

The Basics

Start: Elkview, at Crossings Mall, just off the Elkview exit from I–79.
Length: 42, 83, or 103 miles.
Terrain: Very hilly. Traffic is light on weekend mornings, but during the week it can get heavy with commuter traffic in the mornings and evenings.
Food: Occasional restaurants and convenience stores, but places can be up to 15 miles apart; carry snacks, water, and tools.

Miles & Directions

- 0.0   Turn right out of the parking lot at Crossings Mall onto Rte. 45 (Little Sandy Creek Rd.).
- 6.3   Turn right onto Rte. 119.

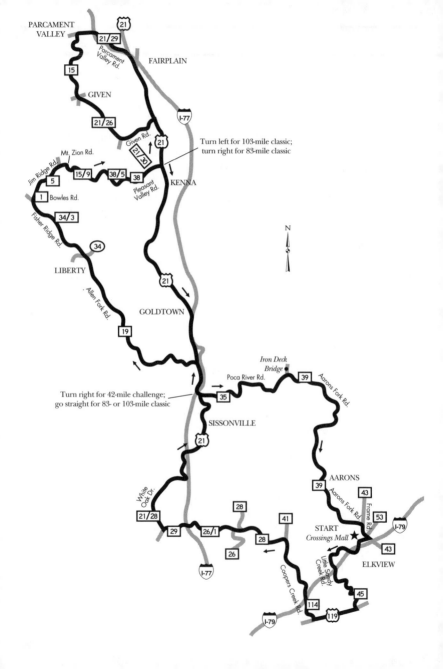

PARCAMENT
VALLEY

21

21/29

Parcament
Valley Rd.

FAIRPLAIN

15

GIVEN

21/26

Given Rd.

21

21/30

I-77

Turn left for 103-mile classic;
turn right for 83-mile classic

Mt. Zion Rd.

Jim Ridge Rd.

15/9   38/5   38

5

KENNA

1   Bowles Rd.

34/3

Pleasant
Valley Rd.

Fisher Ridge Rd.

34

LIBERTY

Allen Fork Rd.

21

GOLDTOWN

19

Iron Deck
Bridge •

Poca River Rd.   39   Aarons Fork Rd.

Turn right for 42-mile challenge;
go straight for 83- or 103-mile classic

35

N

SISSONVILLE

21

AARONS

39   Aarons Fork Rd.

43

White Oak Dr.

53   I-79

21/28

29   26/1   28   41   START
Crossings Mall ★   Frame Rd.

26   28   43

I-77   Coopers Creek Rd.   Little Sandy Creek Rd.   ELKVIEW

114   45

I-79   119

- 8.3   Turn right onto Rte. 114. Here there are a Hardee's and Smith's Grocery Store.

- 9.0   Turn right onto Rte. 41 (Coopers Creek Rd.) and stay on the obvious main road as it changes number from Rte. 41 to Rte. 28 (at mile 12.6, where the road is marked Five Mile Rd.) to Rte. 26 to Rte. 26/1. At mile 13.8 start climbing. At mile 14.2 you'll reach the crest and start a steep downhill. At mile 15.7 start another climb, followed 0.2 mile later by a very steep downhill. Control your speed on the sharp turns.

- 16.8   Bear right at the sharp turn to stay on Rte. 26/1. Watch your speed—the safe maximum is 15 mph.

- 17.5   Turn right onto Rte. 29 (Tuppers Creek Rd.), just before I–77.

- 18.4   Turn left onto Rte. 21/28 (White Oak Dr.); this stretch of the ride is exceptionally scenic. Watch for the sharp S turns on the downhill after mile 19.8.

- 20.1   Turn right onto Rte. 21N. (For a grocery store and restaurant, turn left instead and go 0.7 mile.) At mile 23.8 you'll enter the limits of Sissonville. At mile 25.4 continue straight on Rte. 21 at the intersection of Poca River Rd. (Dolly's convenience store is here.)

  For the 42-mile challenge: At mile 25.4 turn right onto Poca River Rd. (instead of continuing straight) and pick up the directions below at mile 87.5.

- 27.0   Turn left onto Rte. 19 (Allen Fork Rd.), which passes under I–77. At mile 33.5 start a steep but short climb.

- 34.4   Turn left onto Rte. 34S.

- 34.6   Make the first right onto Rte. 34/3 (Fisher Ridge Rd.), passing the Fisher Ridge Winery at mile 37.3. At mile 41.3, be careful! This is the start of a very steep downgrade, which has a stop sign at the bottom.

- 41.7   Turn right onto unmarked Rte. 1 (Bowles Rd.). At mile 41.9 begin climbing.

- 44.4 Bear right at the Y intersection onto Rte. 5 (Jim Ridge Rd.). In 500 feet you can refuel at the Jim Ridge convenience store on your right, where the owner is friendly toward visiting cyclists. *Note:* Between miles 44.7 and 47.0, there are a few gravel sections anywhere from 20 to 100 feet long. Ride with caution!

- 46.2 Turn left at the T intersection onto Mt. Zion Rd. At mile 50.1 continue straight at the intersection of Rock Castle Rd. (Rte. 15/9). After Rock Castle the road you are on will change route numbers several times (from Rte. 15/9 to Rte. 38/5 to Rte. 38 to Rte. 21/30), but continue to follow the evident main road.

- 55.4 Turn left at the T intersection onto Rte. 21N.
  For the 83-mile classic: Turn right onto Rte. 21S instead, and pick up the directions at mile 74.2.

- 57.8 Turn left onto Rte. 21/29 (Given Rd.), which changes to Rte. 38. At mile 62.3 you'll pass through the community of Given, which has no services. Continue north of Given onto Rte. 15.

- 65.6 Bear right at the Y intersection onto Parcament Valley Rd. to Fairplain.

- 66.4 After crossing over I–77, bear right to stay on Parcament Valley Rd. (Rte. 21/26).

- 68.8 Turn right at the T intersection onto Rte. 21S (where there is a convenience store with a small restaurant) and proceed under the interstate. You'll stay on Rte. 21S for the next 18 miles. At mile 71.9 pass the intersection of Given Rd. At mile 74.2 pass the intersection of Pleasant Valley Rd. *This is where the 83-mile classic joins the 103-mile route.* At mile 75.3, just after passing a country store, continue straight as Rte. 34 joins from the left. At mile 76.1 begin climbing Divide Hill. At mile 76.6, at the crest of the hill, continue straight on Rte. 21S where Rte. 34 turns right. Coast down Divide Hill. At mile 82.2 pass under I–77 at Goldtown (a small community with no services). At mile 85.2 pass the intersection of Allen Fork Rd. (Rte. 19) and a convenience store 0.3 mile later.

- 87.5 Turn left onto Rte. 35 (Poca River Rd.). *This is where the 42-mile challenge joins the 103-mile route.* Once again you can refuel at Dolly's convenience store. After crossing Iron Deck Bridge over Hicumbottom Creek, bear right onto Rte. 39 (Aarons Fork Rd.). Use caution on the one-lane bridge at mile 102.2.
- 102.3 Continue straight onto Rte. 43 (Frame Rd.).
- 103.0 Turn right onto Little Sandy Creek Rd., and then make an immediate right into Crossings Mall.

  Congratulations!

24

Observatory and Railroad Classic

Marlinton—Green Bank—Bartow—Cass—
Marlinton

This entire classic is within the Monongahela National Forest, which spreads 848,000 acres over nine counties. The first half of the ride is a 35-mile-long, relatively gentle uphill all the way from Marlinton to Bartow. You'll pass through the Seneca State Forest (304–799–6213), where there is picnicking and primitive camping. The entire ride is within Pocahontas County.

If you don't feel like pedaling the whole 81-mile classic, you can still hit the two main attractions in a shorter challenge of 58 miles, whose cue sheet I devised based on the suggestions of Rachel Alpert, former program director of the Greenbrier River Leadership Center in Bartow (which, among other activities, offers a variety of mountain-bike tours—call 304–456–5191). The entire route was verified by Dennis A. Strawn of Charleston, West Virginia.

The first attraction, some 27 miles into the ride, is the National Radio Astronomy Observatory (NRAO) in Green Bank (304–456–2011). The observatory is open to the public at no charge. You may walk around and gaze at the giant dish-shaped telescopes, which stand in the open air and are used to listen to radio emissions from the heavens twenty-four hours a day. Free tours are given in the summer.

If it is late afternoon when you leave NRAO, you can easily turn the 81-mile classic into a two-day ride by spending the night in Bartow 9 miles north (36 miles into the 81). The nicest place in Bartow is The Hermitage (304–456–4808), a motel and restaurant on the bank of the east fork of the Greenbrier River. The rear door of every room opens onto a long porch, which overlooks a large green and the river—perfect for enjoying a sunset drink and listening to the peepers as the stars come out.

Five miles after leaving Bartow, the second half of the ride becomes almost like mountain biking on pavement: winding, rolling, with rollercoaster-sharp turns and steep climbs, on the appropriately named Back Mountain Road. Also a few miles out of Bartow, check out the Durbin & Greenbrier Valley Railroad (877–MTN–RAIL) along Rte. 250. The railroad offers ninety-minute meandering rides through the Allegheny Highlands and along the Greenbrier River. Farther down, 57 miles into the classic, stop for the second main attraction—a ride on a turn-of-the-century, ninety-ton, steam-powered Shay logging locomotive at the Cass Scenic Railroad State Park (304–456–4300). On selected Saturday evenings throughout the summer you can make reservations on a "dinner train," which includes a barbecue and live bluegrass music.

The last half of the classic, from Bartow through Cass and back to Marlinton, has almost no services. Stock up well at the ride's start in Marlinton, at Green Bank, or at Bartow if you're taking the 58-mile challenge. Route 66 passes The Amish Bakery—an unmarked white farmhouse open Wednesday through Saturday from noon to 5:00 p.m. Don't rely on Cass except during the summer: Even in late May right before Memorial Day, daytime services—including the country store, snack bar, and rest rooms—are closed except for an outdoor soft-drink machine. As there are no bike shops anywhere, be sure to take all the tools you may need.

Marlinton has several places to stay overnight, among them the Marlinton Motor Inn (304–799–4711) and the Jerico B&B (304–799–6241). A night at Marlinton would allow you also to explore the Greenbrier River Hike, Bike, and Ski Trail. The restored railroad depot that is now the Marlinton Visitors Center is an access to the Greenbrier River Trail, the level former bed of the Greenbrier Division of the C&O Railway built at the turn of the century to serve the booming timber industry of the time. Now the public trail passes through numerous small towns and traverses thirty-five bridges and two tunnels, much of the route adjacent to the beautiful Greenbrier River. You can ride along the hard-packed gravel bed as far north as Cass (24 miles) or as far south as North Caldwell (53 miles). For a detailed map and guide to the trail, write to the Greenbrier River Trail Association, Inc., Slatyfork, WV 26291.

The Basics

Start: Marlinton, at the parking lot of the Marlinton Visitors Center (an old converted railroad station) on Rte. 39 0.2 mile east of Rte. 219/15.

Length: 58 or 81 miles.

Terrain: Rolling to hilly. Traffic ranges from moderate to light on the main roads outbound and is practically nonexistent on the return.

Food: Convenience stores and restaurants in Marlinton, Green Bank, and Bartow; food available at Cass between Memorial Day and Labor Day; that is *it!* Moreover, on the 81-mile ride other than in the summer, there could be a stretch of *37 miles without food or water* (from Durbin to Marlinton). Take all necessary tools.

Miles & Directions

- 0.0   Turn left out of the Marlinton Visitors Center parking lot onto Rte. 39E (Main St.). Ride through the quaint, brick downtown district of Marlinton. Load up here on snacks and water;

Durbin & Greenbriar Valley Railroad

DURBIN
BARTOW

west fork

east fork of the Greenbrier River

11 250

The Hermitage

Greenbrier River

National Radio Astronomy Observatory

The Amish Bakery

The Country Store
GREEN BANK

Back Mountain Rd.

CASS

Turn left here for 58-mile challenge; go straight for 90-mile classic

66

66/1

Cass Scenic Railroad State Park

Convenience store

STONY BOTTOM

CLOVER LICK

Back Mountain Rd.

Seneca State Forest

Fairview Rd.

Greenbrier River

N

START
Marlinton Visitor Center

MARLINTON

Airport Rd.

your next opportunity is in 21 miles. After leaving the out-skirts of town, you'll begin climbing.

- 5.2 Turn left onto Rte. 28N, continuing your gradual climb through farm land. At mile 15.5 you'll pass the entrance to the Seneca State Forest.

- 21.0 Turn left at the stop sign to stay on Rte. 28N, where Rte. 92N joins your route. At this intersection are an Exxon gas station and a small convenience store—the first in 21 miles.

- 24.4 At this intersection with Rte. 66W, continue straight to stay on Rte. 28N/92N.

- 27.6 Turn left to enter the grounds of the National Radio Astronomy Observatory. To continue the 81-mile route, leave the observatory grounds by turning left to continue north on Rtes. 28N/92N.

For the 58-mile challenge, leave the observatory grounds by turning right instead and retracing 3.2 miles south along Rte. 28S/92S. Then turn right onto Rte. 66W, coast 4.6 miles down to Cass, and pick up the directions at mile 57.7.

By the way, only 0.6 mile down Rte. 66 from Rtes. 28N/92N is The Amish Bakery; a small sign will direct you to turn right and continue for 0.5 mile. The bakery has a small gravel area for cars to park; walk in the front door and you'll know you've arrived.

- 36.2 Bear left to stay on Rte. 92N/250W as Rte. 28N heads right. You are entering Bartow. Not 500 feet later, just after crossing over the east fork of the Greenbrier River, The Hermitage motel is on your left. At mile 38.9 you'll pass a grocery market in the town of Durbin. At mile 40.0 you'll pass a gas station on your left, which has a small convenience store. This is your *last chance* before Cass—or possibly Marlinton—to stock up on food and drink.

- 40.2 After crossing the west fork of the Greenbrier River, turn left on Grant Vandevender Rd.

- 40.4 Bear right to remain on Grant Vandevender Rd.

- 43.0 Turn left onto Back Mountain Rd. where Rte. 251/11 (Grant Vandevender Rd.) goes straight. This is real backwoods West Virginia, where tumbledown farms with rusting trucks and buses in the muddy yards overlook boulder-strewn fields and forested hills of stunning beauty. Just keep going for nearly 15 miles.

- 57.6 This is Cass. Turn left at the T intersection onto unmarked Rte. 66E. In a few hundred feet you'll be at the Cass County Store and Soda Fountain and Restaurant, the terminus for the scenic railroad in the Cass Scenic Railroad State Park. Across the railroad tracks and to the rear of the parking lot there are picnic tables with barbecue grills on the bank of the Greenbrier River.

- 57.7 To resume the ride turn right out of the Cass Scenic Railroad State Park parking lot onto unmarked Rte. 66W. You'll cross the railroad tracks and pedal through the restored village of Cass, past the rental cabins and gift shops. Cass is also the northernmost access to the Greenbrier River Trail, which is an alternate return to Marlinton (24.6 miles to the south by the trail). You can pick up the Greenbrier River Trail near the Cass Fire Station.

- 59.4 Turn left onto Rte. 1 (Back Mountain Rd.), heading south. At mile 62.5 you'll descend into Stony Bottom, where amid all this wildness you'll suddenly encounter Moore's Lodge Motel (304–456–4721) on your right next to the river; there are no other services. Then you'll begin a very steep climb. At mile 65.4 Rte. 9 (Linwood Rd.) joins Rte. 1 (Back Mountain Rd.) from the right. A mile later you'll enter the small community of Clover Lick—another access to the Greenbrier River Trail for an alternate return to Marlinton (15 miles south by the trail through its most wild and remote section).

- 66.6 Turn right at the T intersection to stay on unmarked Rte. 1/9, following the sign reading marlinton 14 mi. At mile 72.3, stop and enjoy the view for miles around.

- 73.4 Bear right at the Y intersection to stay on Rte. 1 (Back Mountain Rd.) where Rte. 1/6 (Fairview Rd.) heads left.
- 74.1 Turn left at the triangle onto Rte. 15 (Airport Rd.), a two-lane road of excellent pavement that now seems like a veritable freeway. This is a lovely downhill glide past farms.
- 79.5 Turn left at the T intersection onto the unmarked and very busy Rte. 55/219. Watch for cars! If you're hungry, you now have a choice between Kentucky Fried Chicken and Dairy Queen.
- 80.5 Turn left onto Rte. 39E into Marlinton.
- 80.8 Turn left into the parking lot of the Marlinton Visitors Center.

25

Hillsboro Farmland Cruise

Hillsboro—Lobelia—Droop Mountain—Hillsboro

For a true appreciation of West Virginia farmland and country-side, this 25-mile tour in Pocahontas County can't be beat. You'll start in the town of Hillsboro, birthplace of Pearl S. Buck (1892–1973)—the only American woman to be awarded both the Pulitzer Prize in literature (in 1932 for *The Good Earth*) and the Nobel Prize in literature (1938). In fact, just 0.75 mile north of this ride's start on Route 219, the white clapboard home where she was born is now a museum, open to the public Monday through Saturday (for hours call 304–653–4430).

The ride, contributed by the Pocahontas County Tourism Commision and verified by commission administrator Nancy McComb, first meanders through farms where you may see sheep and cattle grazing. But this is no tame and pastoral farmland like the somnolent rolling fields of Pennsylvania. No, this is red-knuckled farmland clinging to the steep sides of hollows, surly in its strong beauty lying naked among the tree-covered rocky hills.

And those rocky hills you will climb. The roads become very twisty, very narrow, and very steep—up to 9 percent grade as you approach and leave Droop Mountain, site of the most extensive Civil War battle in West Virginia. The site is now a state park with a small museum, picnic areas, and a stacked-log lookout tower commanding a spectacular view.

But there's a great payoff for all that climbing: the gorgeous land and its sheer isolation. There is nothing to disturb your contemplation of nature other than the rhythmic sound of your own deep breathing in grinding up switchbacks; in the whole route it is doubtful you'll encounter as many as half a dozen cars (except for the brief stretch on Route 219).

The first half of the ride (up Droop Mountain) is a net climb, with the second half being a net descent, from a high of 3,060 feet above sea level to a low of 2,200 feet. But as in Nepal, there are considerable ups and downs in between; the probable total of a couple of thousand feet gained and lost is the reason this short ride is definitely not a ramble. But it is one of the simplest routes in this book, taking only four roads: Lobelia Road its full length, left onto Route 219 for 2.6 miles, right onto Locust Creek Road for 3 miles, and left onto Denmar Road until its end back in Hillsboro.

These roads are so little traveled that there are *no* services outside of Hillsboro. Stock up there on food and water before you leave, and be sure to take your tools. There are, however, a couple of inns in the area to stay a night: the Yew Mountain Lodge (304–653–4821) and The Current Bed & Breakfast (304–653–4722) halfway through the ride. (The Current, by the way, is adjacent to the Greenbrier River Trail, a generally level former railroad bed now devoted to hiking and biking along the river.) Bicycle campers can pitch a tent and enjoy a hot shower at the 10,000-acre Watoga State Park a few miles northeast of Hillsboro (304–799–4087), http://wvw.com/www/watoga.html.

The Basics

Start: Hillsboro, on Rte. 219 at the corner of Rte. 29 (Lobelia Rd.). Park along Rte. 219 across from the Four Winds Cafe.
Length: 25 miles.
Terrain: Very hilly. Virtually no traffic on the side roads, although traffic may be moderately heavy on the unavoidable 2.6-mile stretch on Rte. 219. *Watch for gravel.*

Food: No services outside of Hillsboro. Take more snacks, water, and tools than you think you might need.

Miles & Directions

- 0.0   From Rte. 219 through the center of Hillsboro, head west (the only direction you can go) onto Rte. 29 (Lobelia Rd.). First you'll ride through open farmland with cows and sheep, and soon you'll be climbing through forest. At mile 4.9 you'll pass Rte. 22 (Russell Scott Rd.) on your left; at mile 6.6 you'll pass Rte. 29/21 (Bruffy's Creek Rd.) on your right. At mile 7.2 follow Rte. 29 (Lobelia Rd.) as it makes a ninety-degree left turn through the town of Lobelia (a few sagging buildings with no services), following the sign TO 219. At mile 8.4 keep heading straight through the intersection of two gravel and dirt roads (George Hill Rd. and Briery Knob Rd.), following the sign TO 219.
- 10.9 Bear left at the unsigned Y intersection to stay on Rte. 29 (Lobelia Rd.). A mile later begin a *steep* climb up the back of Droop Mountain, taking time to enjoy the expansive vista at your left over the valley to forested West Virginia ridges.
- 13.1 Turn left at the T intersection onto Rte. 219. Watch for cars! At this point you are nearly at the summit of the mountain, which has an altitude of 3,060 feet. At mile 13.7 you'll pass one entrance to Droop Mountain State Park on your left. At mile 14.1, after passing a second park entrance, you'll begin a *steep* descent of a 9 percent grade down tight switchbacks for the next 0.75 mile. *Caution! Watch for gravel and cars!*
- 15.7 Turn right onto Rte. 20 (Locust Creek Rd.).
- 18.8 Turn left at the T intersection onto unmarked Rte. 31 (Denmar Rd.). But before you make the turn, you might want to detour 100 feet to your right to walk through the century-old covered bridge, no longer in service for automobile traffic but preserved for posterity as a landmark.

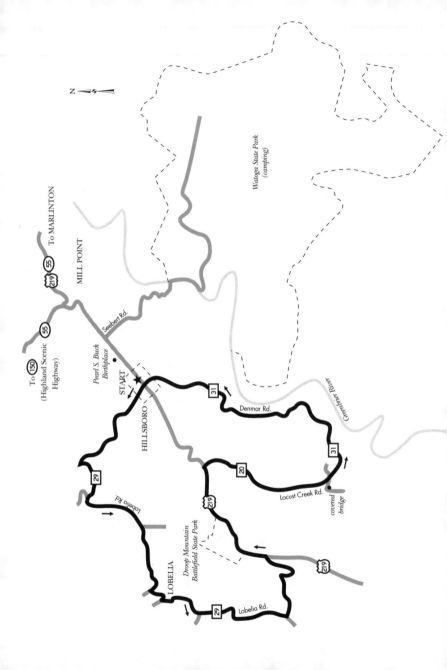

N

To MARLINTON

55 219

55

To 150
(Highland Scenic
Highway)

MILL POINT

Seebert Rd.

Watoga State Park
(camping)

Pearl S. Buck
Birthplace

START

HILLSBORO

31

Denmar Rd.

31

20

Greenbrier River

Locust Creek Rd.

covered
bridge

29

Lobelia Rd.

219

Droop Mountain
Battlefield State Park

219

LOBELIA

29

Lobelia Rd.

219

- 20.1 Bear left at the small white church to stay on Rte. 31 (Denmar Rd.). At mile 20.7 you'll have descended to the lowest point on the ride, 2,200 feet. The rest is a relatively gentle ascent.
- 21.4 Turn right at the T intersection to stay on unmarked Rte. 31 (Denmar Rd.). Now you're pedaling through farmland.
- 25.1 Arrive back at Rte. 219 at your starting point, across the highway from Rte. 29 (Lobelia Rd.). (To visit the Pearl S. Buck Birthplace, turn right onto Rte. 219 and ride another 0.75 mile.)

26

West Virginia Mountain Classic

Slatyfork—Spruce Knob—Watoga State Park—Seneca State Forest—Slatyfork

Climbing and winding its way through some of the highest and best preserved country east of the Mississippi River, the West Virginia Mountain Classic is an outdoor adventure for the conditioned cyclist looking for a challenge. This 97-mile ride begins in one of the East's top mountain biking and downhill skiing towns before crossing one of West Virginia's highest peaks and continuing through a wilderness area, a national forest, a state forest, and state park. Along the way, riders will also pass the birthplace of author Pearl S. Buck and the small country towns of Hillsboro, Seebert, Huntersville, and Edray. And given the area's 7,000-feet-plus elevation, even summer riding is filled with cool breezes, low humidity, and relatively few biting insects.

The abundance of state and national forest land also offers some of the East Coast's best back-country camping, hiking, fishing, and skiing.

Riders will begin this classic at the Elk River Inn and Restaurant (Touring Center) (304) 572–3771, which has served as a base camp and touring center for cyclists of the off-road variety for more than 20 years. The center, in Slatyfork, provides extensive tours and training for mountain bikers and is home to the fifteen-year-old West Virginia Fat Tire Festival. (Also, just a few miles north of the center, is the Snowshoe Mountain resort (304) 572–5252, which, in addition to top-flight winter skiing, also offers extensive mountain biking trails.)

Staying firmly on paved ground, however, this tour leaves the center and continues along the edge of Scenic Highway 150. This highway, similar to the well-known Blue Ridge Parkway, provides great long-range mountain views and passes over the 7,703-foot-elevation Red Spruce Knob overlook. You'll then continue to the unspoiled lands of the Cranberry Wilderness Area as you cut through the Monogahela National Forest (304) 846–2695.

The route continues up and over Sugar Creek Mountain, Black Mountain, and Little Mountain before reaching the Watoga State Park (304) 799–4087 and the ride's halfway point. The park is a little more developed than the surrounding area and offers a restaurant, visitors center, and swimming pool.

You'll then ride north to the Seneca State Forest (304) 799–6213 before turning west toward the town of Edray and back to the Elk River Touring Center.

This is the book's most challenging ride. Its climbs are long and its downhills are fast. And though small towns and various visitor's centers are located about every 30 miles, the areas in between are often isolated and with a phone in walking distance. Accommodations, except for the touring center and a few small towns, are forests and if you don't think you'll be able to complete this century in a single day, you'll need to bring overnight camping gear or arrange for accommodations in one of the small towns.

A multi-day ride should also involve pre-planning, including contacting the local forest office to reserve campsites and discuss available services.

Cyclists attempting this route should have some touring and camping experience as well as mechanical skills to handle problems along the way. Review "A Special Word about West Virginia" in this book's Introduction to learn more about the unique challenge of road touring in this mountain state.

For more information about accommodations or services call the Pocahontas County Tourism Bureau at (800) 336–7009.

This ride was designed and verified by Gil Willis, co-owner of the Elk River Touring Center.

The Basics

Start: Elk River Touring Center, Slatyfork, WV. From Pennsylvania, take I–81S to Rte. 33W. Follow Rte. 33W to Rte. 28 in West Virginia. Turn left onto Rte. 28 and follow through the town of Cass, WV, where you will turn right onto WV Rte. 66. Follow Rte. 66 to Hwy. 219. Turn left on Rte. 219. The Elk River Inn and Restaurant (Touring Center) will be five miles ahead on your right. From Richmond, VA, take I–64W to the Stanton, VA, exit. Turn right at the bottom of the exit through downtown Stanton. Turn right onto Rte. 254, which will run into Rte. 42S. Follow Rte. 42S to the town of Goshen, VA, where you will bear right onto Rte. 39. Follow Rte. 39 to Marlinton, where you will turn right onto Hwy. 219. The Elk River Inn and Restaurant (Touring Center) will be 15 miles north on your left.

Length: 96.9 miles.

Terrain: This is the book's most difficult ride. It is for conditioned and experienced cyclists. A good deal of endurance is needed to conquer its many climbs, and fine-tuned handling skills are a must to safely navigate its quick downhill runs. Mountain Challenge riders should also possess basic repair skills to handle mechanical problems along isolated sections.

Food: Bring your own snacks and water as food and rest rooms are scarce along this rural mountain ride. Food and facilities are available, however, at the Elk River Touring Center, the town of Hillsboro (roughly mile 40), Seebert (mile 42), the Watoga State Park (mile 46) and in the town of Huntersville (mile 58).

Miles & Directions

- 0.0   Turn right out of the Elk River Touring Center onto Hwy. 219.

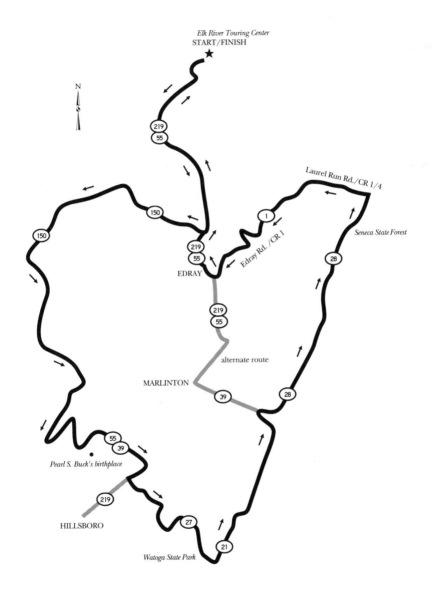

Elk River Touring Center
START/FINISH

N

219
55

Laurel Run Rd./CR 1/4

150

1

Seneca State Forest

150

219
55

28

EDRAY

Edray Rd./CR 1

219
55

alternate route

MARLINTON

39

28

55
39

Pearl S. Buck's birthplace

219

HILLSBORO

27

21

Watoga State Park

- 8.2   Turn right onto Scenic Hwy. 150.
  Note: To reduce this 97-mile loop by 16.4 miles, begin and end your ride in the parking lot provided here at the start of Scenic Hwy. 150.
- 18.0 Cross the Williams River Bridge. You'll begin a 5-mile climb to the Big Spruce overlook.
- 18.3 You'll pass the Tea Campground, where water is available.
- 31.7 Turn left onto Rte. 55 (Rte. 39) toward Millpoint.
- 38.3 Turn right onto Hwy. 219 and follow the signs to Watoga State Park. The park has drinking water, rest rooms, and a restaurant. The park also offers nature trails, a small lake, and a pool.
- 39.7 Turn left onto Seebert Rd. (County Rd. 27). Cross the Greenbrier River Trail and the Greenbrier River.
  Note: To reach author Pearl Buck's birthplace and the town of Hillsboro, continue straight on Hwy. 219 an additional mile rather than turning onto Seebert Rd. (County Rd. 27). Continue an additional 2 miles to reach the Hillsboro country store with deli. To resume the ride, follow Hwy. 219 the way you came and turn right onto Seebert Rd. (County Rd. 27).
- 42.8 Bear left at a fork in the road and begin a steep climb into the Watoga State Park.
- 46.4 Bear left at a second fork to remain on County Rd. 27. You'll pass the Watoga Park office, which provides information and phone service.
- 48.7 Turn left at the T intersection onto unmarked County Rd. 21. You will see a sign for the town of Huntersville at this intersection.
- 56.1 Turn left onto State Rd. 39W.
- 57.0 Turn right onto State Rd. 28N. You'll pass Pocahontas County High School and the Seneca State Forest. A small grocery store is located in Huntersville.
  Note: For a shorter but steep ride of 80 miles, continue straight on State Rd. 39 rather than turning onto State Rd. 28. Follow State Rd. 39 into Marlington, where you will turn right onto Hwy. 219 and

begin the long climb back to the Elk River Touring Center. Remember, this option maybe shorter, but it's just as tough.

- 69.9 Turn left onto Laurel Run Rd. (County Rd. 1/4). Follow Laurel Run (County Rd. 1/4) into downtown Cloverlick. You'll cross again over the Greenbriar River Trail and past the trail's old train depot on your left. Laurel Run will become scenic Edray Rd. (County Rd. 1) in the town of Edray. (Locals refer to this road as Back Mountain Rd.)
- 85.0 Turn right onto Hwy. 219 to begin the climb back up to Scenic Hwy. 150.
- 88.7 Cross Hwy. 150 and continue north on Hwy. 219.
- 96.9 Arrive back at the Elk River Touring Center.

27

West Virginia Inn to Inn Ramble

Elkins—Beverly—Dailey—Mill Creek—Huttonsville

Few things are as romantic as a quiet country inn. But a majestic bike ride for two through the beautiful West Virginia mountains comes pretty close.

The West Virginia Inn to Inn Ramble has put the two together for what has proven to be a relaxing and athletic two-day get away. The ride begins at the quaint, five-room colonial Warfield House Bed & Breakfast (888) 636–4555 in the town of Elkins, West Virginia. Elkins is a small country hamlet situated in the middle of some of the East Coast's best-known outdoor areas. The top-notch skiing of Canaan Valley Resort State Park (304) 866–4121 and the Timberline Resort (304) 866–4777 is a forty-five-minute drive west. While much of the East's best rock climbing and West Virginia's highest point are located one hour east in the Spruce Knob area.

A one-hour trek south will take you to the Elk River Touring Center (304) 572–3771 and some of the state's top mountain-biking trails.

Because of its central location, the Inn to Inn Ramble can stand alone as part of a gentle, two-day escape or as the start of a longer outdoor adventure.

After leaving the Warfield Inn, the ride travels a couple of miles along Elkins' small town roads before heading out into the real countryside and some great mountain views.

The route follows a relatively quiet country road, which straddles and many times crosses sections of the lazy Tygart River. The ride passes rural towns that have gone largely unchanged since the days when small towns were the rule. You can take a detour to the antique shops and Civil War museum of Beverly or try country cooking in the restaurants of Dailey and Valley Bend.

The first half of the ride ends in the town of Huttonsville and the Queen Anne Victorian–style Hutton House Bed & Breakfast (304) 335–6701. The small, six-room inn has been meticulously restored since it was purchased by the honeymooning couple of Loretta Murray and Dean Ahren in 1987. The Inn sits atop Huttonsville and offers broad views of the Tygart River and the Laurel Mountains.

Though West Virginia, as mentioned earlier in this book, can prove to be a difficult place to ride even for conditioned cyclists, this two-day ramble is among the less exhausting and technical of the state's road-cycling tours. It can be hilly in spots and requires riders to be in fairly good shape; however, only one of the many folks who have taken this trip has said it was too difficult, said Connie Garnett, who owns the Warfield Inn and designed this ride.

For more information about cycling in West Virginia call the state tourism bureau at (800) CALL–WVA.

The Basics

Start: Warfield House, Buffalo Street, Elkins, WV. From Washington, D.C., take Interstate 66W to Interstate 81S. Take your second exit, which will be Strasburg/Rte. 55. Turn right after exiting to follow Rte. 55 to Rte. 33W. Turn right onto Rte. 33W and drive to Elkins. Turn right again in Elkins to remain on Rte. 33. Drive 2 more miles and turn right onto an unmarked road at the Iron Horse statue. The Warfield House will be 200 yards ahead on your right. From Pittsburgh, PA, take Interstate 79S to exit 99, which will be Rte. 33E. Follow Rte. 33E into Elkins where you'll turn left at the Iron Horse statue. The Warfield House will be 200 yards ahead on your right.

Length: 47.2 miles (23.6 miles each way).

Terrain: This ride is moderately hilly and will test the stamina of those who don't ride often. On the other hand, the ride is largely a straight along lightly traveled roads with few technical skills required and plenty of places to rest.

Food: Food and rest rooms are available at both inns, as well in the small towns at miles 9.7, 14.3, and 18.4. A grocery store is located along the route at mile 22.1.

Miles & Directions

- 0.0   Turn left out of the Warfield House (888) 636–4555 onto Sycamore St.
- 0.2   Cross Randolph Ave. where you will bear immediately left onto Kearns Ave.
- 0.6   Turn right onto Third St.
- 0.8   Turn left at the traffic light onto Davis Ave.
- 1.8   Bear right onto South Gate Rd.
- 1.9   Turn right at the stop sign onto an unmarked road. Jennings Randolph Elementary School will be directly in front of you.
- 2.0   Turn left onto Georgetown Rd.
- 2.5   Continue straight on Georgetown Rd. past the International Order of Odd Fellows.
- 2.9   Cross an unmarked bridge over a small section of the Tygart River.

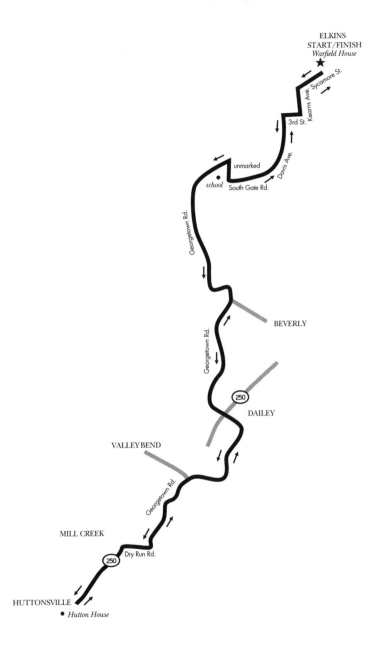

ELKINS
START/FINISH
Warfield House

Sycamore St.

Kearns Ave.

3rd St.

Davis Ave.

unmarked

school

South Gate Rd.

Georgetown Rd.

BEVERLY

Georgetown Rd.

250

DAILEY

VALLEY BEND

Georgetown Rd.

MILL CREEK

250

Dry Run Rd.

HUTTONSVILLE

Hutton House

- 3.5   Pass a sign indicating the site of county tractor sales.
- 4.5   Pass a mail box with the name Cowgill across the top.
- 5.5   Coast down a slight incline.
- 5.8   Note the quaint yellow spring house up the hill to your right.
- 6.1   Pass the private home known as Pingley's Poverty Acres on your left.
- 6.5   Watch for a mailbox topped with a model C-130 airplane.
- 7.1   An interesting circa 1800s home, white and narrow with a red roof, will be on your left.
- 8.2   Also on your left will be an picturesque log cabin with a pond.
- 9.5   Again cross the Tygart River after a winding section of road.
- 9.7   Turn left at the stop sign to remain on Georgetown Rd.
  Note: To enter the town of Beverly, which features a Civil War museum, antique shops, historic homes, and a restaurant, do not turn left here but continue straight for approximately 1 mile. After visiting Beverly, turn around and head back to Georgetown Rd. to continue the ride.
- 10.2 Turn right at the stop sign to continue on Georgetown Rd.
- 10.7 Note the brown house on your left.
- 11.2 Watch for the stone house on your right. Farther down you'll also pass a green-sided metal barn.
- 14.1 You'll pass the New Deal Era Homestead Houses. The community was built as a cooperative experiment in which the U.S. Government and homeowners constructed the houses together and clusters of homes were required to work together to provide income for the community.
- 14.3 Bear left across Rte. 250 as Georgetown Rd. becomes County Rd. 39 heading into the town of Dailey.

Note: You are about half way through the first day's ride, so the Country Roads Family Restaurant (304) 338–2515 in Dailey might be a good place to stop for lunch.

- 14.8 Leave Dailey and cross the Tygart River.
- 15.6 You'll pass an interesting Victorian-style home.
- 15.4 Continue straight through the stop sign.
- 17.7 Pass a sign for McGee Rd.
- 18.4 Bear left beside—but do not cross—a metal bridge.
  Note: To reach the town of Valley Bend and the homestyle cooking of Cherry and Janice's Restaurant (304) 338–4545, bear left across the metal bridge onto an unmarked road and continue straight for less than a mile. Turn left onto Rte. 250. The restaurant is just past the intersection. Retrace your steps to County Rd. 39 to continue the ride.
- 19.2 Coast down a small incline and cross another bridge.
- 19.6 The road will begin to wind as you pass a small pond.
- 20.6 Note the old, weathered barn to your right
- 21.5 Bear right at a fork in the road onto Dry Run Rd.
- 21.7 Enter the town of Mill Creek.
- 22.0 Pass a baseball field and community park on your right.
- 22.1 You're almost to the Hutton Inn, but if you really need a drink, stop at this grocery store.
- 22.4 Turn left at the Mill Creek Presbyterian Church onto Rte. 250.
- 23.0 Pass the entrance sign for the town of Huttonsville.
- 23.6 Arrive at the Hutton House (800) 234–6701.

Appendix

Below are some selected references pertinent to bicycle touring in the Mid-Atlantic. The list is not exhaustive. If any organization, set of maps, or other helpful reference has been omitted or information has changed, please send the necessary information to the author for inclusion in the next edition of this book: Patrick M. Gilsenan, c/o The Globe Pequot Press, P.O. Box 480, Guilford, CT 06437 (email: ptgilsenan@aol.com).

National Cycling Organizations

Adventure Cycling Association
P.O. Box 8308
Missoula, MT 59807
(406) 721–1776

The Adventure Cycling Association is national non-profit organization representing recreational cyclists founded in 1973. The organization has helped establish the 24,000-mile National Bicycle Route Network, for which it publishes maps and marks cross-state and cross-country roads as bicycle routes. The association's members receive nine yearly editions of *Adventure Cyclist* and an annual *Cyclists' Yellow Pages*. The organization also sells tents, guidebooks, and touring merchandise, and conducts cross-country, guided bicycle tours up to three months long.

League of American Bicyclists
1612 K St., NW, Suite 401
Washington, D.C. 20006
(202) 822–1333

The League (a century-old organization formerly known as the League of American Wheelmen) is a national, non-profit organization representing the interests of commuting, touring, and recreational cyclists. The full-time League staff works with Congress and local communities to insure continued funding for cyclists and to help communities use those funds effectively. The League also publishes the annual *Almanac of Bicycling* and six yearly editions of the magazine *Bicycle USA*.

National Center for Bicycling and Walking
1506 21st Street, NW, Ste. 200
Washington, D.C. 20036
(202) 463–6622
www.bikefed.org

The Center for Bicycling and Walking (formerly the Bicycle Federation of America) is a national non-profit dedicated to helping municipalities construct, develop, and maintain more walkable and rideable communities.

Rails to Trails Conservancy
1100 17th St., NW
Washington, DC 20036
(202) 331–9696
Fax: (202) 331–9680
www.railtrails.org

The Rails to Trails Conservancy is a national non-profit dedicated to converting unused railroad corridors into multi-use public trails. The nation's better-known rail trails have become popular commuter routes as well as jogging, roller blading, and general recreation destinations.

State Bicycle and Pedestrian Coordinators

State Bicycle and Pedestrian Coordinators are state government positions mandated by the U.S. Congress as part of the last two national transportation bills. These coordinators are responsible for drafting statewide plans for bicycle use within each state's recreation and commuting structures. A good coordinator will know as much or more than anyone about cycling in the state.

Delaware

Delaware Bicycle Council
c/o Elizabeth Holloway
P.O. Box 778 Dover, DE 19903
(302) 760–BIKE
www. state.de.us/del./bike

Maryland

Harvey J. Muller
Bicycle & Pedestrian Crdn.
Maryland State Highway Administration
707 North Calvert St.
P.O. Box 717
Baltimore, MD 21203–0717
(410) 545–5656 or
(800) 252–8776
e-mail:
hmuller@sha.state.md.us

Washington, D.C.

Gilbert Williams
Bicycle & Pedestrian Crdnr.
D.C. Dept. of Public Works
2000 14th. St., NW, 5th Floor
Washington, D.C. 20009
(202) 671–0537

Virginia

Ken Lantz
Virginia Dept. of Transportation
Office of State Bicycle &
Pedestrain Program
1401 E. Broad Street
Richmond, VA 23219
(804) 371–4869 or
(800) 835–1203
www.vdot.state.va.us
e-mail:
vabiking@vdot.state.va.us

West Virginia

Dave Cramer
Bicycle & Pedestrian Crdnr.
WV DOT Division of Highways
1900 Kanawha St., East
Building 5, Room A-816
Charleston, WV 25305–0430
(304) 558–3113
e-mail:
dcramer@dot.state.wv.us

State Cycling Advocacy and Recreation Clubs

Delaware

White Clay Bicycle Club
c/o Dave Green
3 Yale Road, Cooper Farm
Wilmington, DE 19808
(302) 994–2990
www.delanet.com/~wcbc/

Maryland

Annapolis Bicycle Club, Inc.
P.O. Box 224
Annapolis, MD 21404
(410) 295–5144
www.annapolis.net/abc

Baltimore Bicycling Club
P.O. Box 5894
Baltimore,MD 21282
(410) 7928308

Chesapeake Wheelmen
P.O. Box 9372
Baltimore,MD 21228
(410) 247–4064
www.chesapeakewheelmen.org

Virginia

A. P. Hill/Rappahannock
Bicycle Club
c/o James S. Day, Jr.
P.O. Box 682
Bowling Green, VA 22427
(804) 633–5132

Eastern Tandem Rally, Inc.
c/o Bob Friedman
5514 Callander Dr.
Springfield,VA 22151–0402
(703) 978–7937

Fredericksburg Cyclists
P.O. Box 7844
Fredericksburg, VA 22404
(540) 373–1451

Potomac Pedalers Touring Club
6878 Fleetwood Rd., Suite D
McLean, VA 22101
(703) 442–8780

Reston Bicycle Club
P.O. Box 3389

Reston, VA 20195
(703) 904–0900

Shenandoah Valley Bicycle
Club
c/o Marcia Lamphier
P.O. Box 1014
Harrisonburg, VA 22801–1014
(540) 289–6712
e-mail: neups@shentel.net

Washington, DC
Washington Area Bicyclist Association (WABA)
633 15th Street, NW, Suite 1030
Washington, D.C. 20005

(202) 628–2500
www.waba.org
e-mail: waba@waba.org

West Virginia
Mountain State Wheelers
Bicycle Club
P.O. Box 8161
South Charleston, WV 25303
(304) 345–5886

Tri-State Wheelers
c/o Darin Evans
156 Lynnwood Manor Apt.
Weirton, WV 26061
(304) 723–3668

Bicycle Touring Companies

This is a partial list of locally based commercial touring companies that concentrate their efforts in the Mid-Atlantic. Many reputable touring companies headquatered outside the area also offer Mid-Atlantic tours. For more information consult the Adventure Cycling Association's *The Cyclists' Yellow Pages*.

Appalachian Valley Bicycle Touring
31 East Fort Ave.
Baltimore, MD 21230
(410) 837–8068
Maryland, Pennsylvania, and West Virginia tours

Bike the Sites, Inc.
Washington, D.C.

(202) 966–8662
www.bikethesites.com
Maryland, Virginia, and greater Washington, D.C. tours

Elk River Touring Center
8C69 Box 16
Slatyfork, WV 26291
(304) 572–3771
www.ertc.com
West Virginia mountain bike tours

Old Dominion Bicycle Tours
3620 Huguenot Trail
Powhatan,VA 23139
(804) 598–1808 or
(888) 296–5036
www.olddominianbike.qpg.com
Rural and historic Virginia tours

Wayfarers
P.O. Box 15671
Washington, D.C. 20003
(202) 234–2524
Mid-Atlantic and international
tours

State Bicycling Maps and Guides

National Rails-to-Trails
Conservancy
National Headquarters
1100 17th St., NW, 10th Floor
Washington, D.C. 20036
(202) 331–9696
www.railtrails.org

DeLorme Mapping Company
P.O. Box 298
2 DeLorme Drive
Yarmouth, ME 04096
(800) 452–5931
www.DeLorme.com
Offers an *Atlas & Gazetteer* for
all fifty states. The large-format
book of topographic maps also
shows dirt and paved roads and
suggested bicycle routes. It also
lists wildlife areas and other
local attractions. These maps
are accurate and superb in rural
areas. Their scale is too small,
however, to be helpful in towns
and cities. For a map list and
prices, contact DeLorme Mapping Company at the above address and telephone number.

Delaware Contract Admin.
Delaware Dept. of Transportation
P.O. Box 778
Dover, DE 19903
(302) 760–2495
Offers 23 x 30-inch, 1997 map
identifying statewide bicycle
routes.

Maryland Highway
Information Services
Division 707 North Calvert
Street
Mail Stop C-607
Baltimore, MD 21202
(410) 545–8747
www.sha.state.md.us
e-mail: mmcneill@
sha.state.md.us

Bicycle & Pedestrian
Coordinator
Maryland State Highway
Administration
707 North Calvert St.
P.O. Box 717
Baltimore, MD 21203–0717
(410) 545–5656 or
(800) 252–8776
e-mail:
hmuller@sha.state.md.us

Tourism Council of Frederick
County, Inc.

19 E. Church Street
Frederick, MD 21701
(301) 663–8687 or
(800) 999–3613
Offers maps for $4 plus tax at the visitors center or $5.70 by mail.

Carroll County Visitor Center
210 E. Main St.
Westminster, MD 21157
(800) 272–1933
Offers free cue sheets and maps for ten bicycle tours in Carroll County.

Chesapeake & Ohio Canal Maps
C & O Canal Ntl. Historic Park
P.O. Box 4
Sharpsburg, MD 21782
(301) 739–4200
Offers free map of 184.5-mile bicycle and hiking trail along the canal towpath from Cumberland, MD, to Washington, D.C.

Washington, D.C.

D.C. Committee to Promote Washington
1212 New York Avenue, NW, Suite 200
Washington, D.C. 20005
(202) 724–5644
www.washington.org

ADC, "The Map People"
6440 General Green Way
Alexandria,VA 22312
(703) 750–0510
www.adcmap.com

Offers a 1998 map compiled by the Metropolitan Washington Council of Governments covering major named trails, parking areas, road bike routes, unofficial bike routes, trail etiquette, and safety as well as public transportation access and regulations. $8.95 for fifth edition (1998) map.

Washington Area Bicyclist Association (WABA)
633 15th Street, NW, Suite 1030
Washington, DC 20005
(202) 628–2500
www.waba.org
e-mail: waba@waba.org
Offers maps of sixty-seven rides, noting historical sights and places to stop for refreshments in Delaware, Washington, D.C., Maryland, Pennsylvania, Virginia and West Virginia. Fifth edition, 1998, $16.95 plus $3.75 shipping and handling.

Virginia

Virginia Department of Transportation
Information Office
1401 E. Broad St.
Richmond, VA 23219
(804) 786–2801
Offers fold-up county maps with a scale of 1 inch to 2 miles. $.50 per map plus tax.

Northern Virginia Regional
Park Authority
5400 Ox Rd.
Fairfax, VA 22039
(703) 729–0596 or (703)
352–5900
Offers trail guide to the Washington & Old Dominion Railroad Regional Park.

West Virginia

West Virginia County Maps
and Recreational Guide
N. 2445 County Road HH
Lyndon Station, WV 53944
(608) 666–3331
Offers fifty-five county maps
with list of state parks and
natural areas. $16.85 including
shipping.

Elk River Touring Center
8C69 Box 16
Slatyfork, WV 26291
(304) 572–3771
www.ertc.com
Offers maps of the 75-mile
Greenbrier River Trail, which is
an unpaved railroad right-of-
way along the Greenbrier
River. The maps feature access
points and accommodations.
$2 plus postage. Also offers a
$9 dollar waterproof *Slatyfork
Trail Guide* that topographi-
cally maps eight easy to expert
level, Slatyfork-area mountain
biking trails.

Additional Mid-Atlantic Cycling Resources

The tabloid-size newspaper
Spokes, published ten times a
year, covers bicycle touring,
racing, off-road recreation,
triathlon, and commuting
news in the Mid-Atlantic
states. It is available for free at
many area bicycle stores, fitness centers, and sporting establishments in Maryland,
Virginia, Washington, D.C.,
and parts of Delaware, Pennsylvania, and West Virginia.
For more information, contact
editor and publisher Neil W.
Sandler at *Spokes*, 5334
Sovereign Pl., Frederick, MD
21710, (301) 846–0326.